TEACHING GOLF

Steps to Success

DeDe Owens, EdD
Teaching Professional
Cog Hill Golf & Country Club
Lemont, Illinois

Linda K. Bunker, PhD
Professor, Curry School of Education
University of Virginia, Charlottesville

Leisure Press
Champaign, Illinois

Library of Congress Cataloging-in-Publication Data

Owens, DeDe.
  Teaching golf: steps to success / DeDe Owens, Linda K. Bunker.
    p.   cm.—(Steps to success activity series)
  Bibliography: p.
  ISBN 0-88011-322-7
  1. Golf—Study and teaching.   I. Bunker, Linda K.   II. Title.
  III. Series.
  GV965.O88   1989
  796.352'307—dc19   88-648
                                                      CIP

Developmental Editor: Judy Patterson Wright, PhD
Production Director: Ernie Noa
Copy Editor: Peter Nelson
Assistant Editors: Kathy Kane, Steve Otto, and Christine Drews
Proofreader: Laurie McGee
Typesetter: Yvonne Winsor
Text Design: Keith Blomberg
Text Layout: Tara Welsch
Cover Design: Jack Davis
Cover Photo: Bill Morrow
Illustrations By: Raneé Rogers and Gretchen Walters
Printed By: Phillips Brothers Printers

ISBN: 0-88011-322-7

Printed in the United States of America

10 9 8 7 6 5 4 3 2 1

Leisure Press
A Division of Human Kinetics Publishers, Inc.
Box 5076, Champaign, IL 61820
1-800-342-5457
1-800-334-3665 (in Illinois)

Contents

Series Preface

The Steps to Success Activity Series is a breakthrough in skill instruction through the development of complete learning progressions—the *steps to success*. These *steps* help students quickly perform basic skills successfully and prepare them to acquire advanced skills readily. At each step, students are encouraged to learn at their own pace and to integrate their new skills into the total action of the activity, which motivates them to achieve.

The unique features of the Steps to Success Activity Series are the result of comprehensive development—through analyzing existing activity books, incorporating the latest research from the sport sciences and consulting with students, instructors, teacher educators, and administrators. This groundwork pointed up the need for three different types of books—for participants, instructors, and teacher educators—which we have created and together comprise the Steps to Success Activity Series.

The *participant book* for each activity is a self-paced, step-by-step guide; learners can use it as a primary resource for a beginning activity class or as a self-instructional guide. The unique features of each *step* in the participant book include

- sequential illustrations that clearly show proper technique for all basic skills,
- helpful suggestions for detecting and correcting errors,
- excellent drill progressions with accompanying *Success Goals* for measuring performance, and
- a complete checklist for each basic skill for a trained observer to rate the learner's technique.

A comprehensive *instructor guide* accompanies the participant's book for each activity, emphasizing how to individualize instruction. Each *step* of the instructor's guide promotes successful teaching and learning with

- teaching cues (*Keys to Success*) that emphasize fluidity, rhythm, and wholeness,

- criterion-referenced rating charts for evaluating a participant's initial skill level,
- suggestions for observing and correcting typical errors,
- tips for group management and safety,
- ideas for adapting every drill to increase or decrease the difficulty level,
- quantitative evaluations for all drills (*Success Goals*), and
- a complete test bank of written questions.

The series textbook, *Instructional Design for Teaching Physical Activities*, explains the *steps to success* model, which is the basis for the Steps to Success Activity Series. Teacher educators can use this text in their professional preparation classes to help future teachers and coaches learn how to design effective physical activity programs in school, recreation, or community teaching and coaching settings.

After identifying the need for participant, instructor, and teacher educator texts, we refined the *steps to success* instructional design model and developed prototypes for the participant and the instructor books. Once these prototypes were fine-tuned, we carefully selected authors for the activities who were not only thoroughly familiar with their sports but had years of experience in teaching them. Each author had to be known as a gifted instructor who understands the teaching of sport so thoroughly that he or she could readily apply the *steps to success* model.

Next, all of the participant and instructor manuscripts were carefully developed to meet the guidelines of the *steps to success* model. Then our production team, along with outstanding artists, created a highly visual, user-friendly series of books.

The result: The Steps to Success Activity Series is the premier sports instructional series available today. The participant books are the best available for helping you to become a master player, the instructor guides will help you to become a master teacher, and the teacher educator's text prepares you to design your own programs.

This series would not have been possible without the contributions of the following:

- Dr. Joan Vickers, instructional design expert,
- Dr. Rainer Martens, Publisher,
- the staff of Human Kinetics Publishers, and

- the *many* students, teachers, coaches, consultants, teacher educators, specialists, and administrators who shared their ideas—and dreams.

Judy Patterson Wright
Series Editor

Preface

To be a successful golf instructor you need to understand the golf swing, be able to communicate the swing mechanics to your students, and be able to observe its characteristics in order to identify errors and potential strategies for correction. The material presented in this book provides a systematic way to help you become that successful instructor.

The philosophy behind this book is based on the assumption that learning occurs through progressive steps that build one upon another. In addition, the principle of active learning is advocated through the use of many partner activities that are structured to provide students the means to be self-correctors. Through learning to be good observers of golf, students will be better able to participate in effective learning experiences. The checklists, drills, and teaching techniques are designed to help focus attention on the process of learning a technical, sound golf swing as well as producing effective performance, resulting in lower scores on the golf course.

The teaching styles and learning experiences provided in this book include the full spectrum of techniques from command to discovery.

The mixture of teaching styles and exciting learning activities will allow for the greatest growth of each student. The best way for this learning to occur is to establish a shared responsibility with your students. By giving up some control, you can help them take control of their own learning. After all, you can not be there all the time, so you must help them be self-teachers, by learning to use the Checklists and Keys to Success provided in each area.

As teachers ourselves, we have observed and utilized these techniques with a variety of learners of every age and skill from professional golfers and athletes to preschool children. We are pleased to be able to share these ideas with other teachers and wish to thank Human Kinetics Publishers and Dr. Judith Wright for making the series ''Steps to Success'' a reality. Through this series, we believe that teachers will be prepared to provide optimal golf instruction.

DeDe Owens
Linda Bunker

Implementing the Steps to Success Staircase

This book is meant to be flexible not only to your students' needs but to your needs as well. It is common to hear that students' perceptions of a task change as the task is learned. However, we often forget that teachers' perceptions and actions also change (Goc-Karp & Zakrajsek, 1987; Housner & Griffey, 1985; Imwold & Hoffman, 1983).

More experienced or master teachers tend to approach the teaching of activities in a similar manner. They are highly organized (e.g., they do not waste time getting groups together or use long explanations); they integrate information (e.g., from biomechanics, kinesiology, exercise physiology, motor learning, sport psychology, cognitive psychology, instructional design, etc.); and they relate basic skills into the larger game or performance context. This includes succinctly explaining why the basic skills, concepts, or tactics are important within the game or performance setting. Then, usually within a few minutes, their students are placed into game-like practice situations that progress in steps that follow logical manipulations of factors such as

- the length of the swing (1 to 1, 2 to 2, 3 to 3, 4 to 4, 5 to 5),
- the direction of the target,
- the lie of the ball,
- the placement of the ball in the stance,
- the tension in various body parts, and
- the size and distance of targets.

This book will show you how the basic golf skills, tactics, and selected physiological, psychological, and other pertinent knowledge are interrelated (see Appendix A for an overview). You can use this information not only to gain insights into the various interrelationships but also to define the subject matter for golf. The following questions offer specific suggestions for implementing this knowledge base and help you to evaluate and improve your teaching methods, which include class organiza-

tion, drills, objectives, progressions, and evaluations.

1. Under what conditions do you teach?
   - How much space is available?
   - What type of equipment is available? It may be necessary to construct some of your own equipment. See Appendix B for a list of instructional aids, their purposes, and design suggestions.
   - What is the average class size?
   - How much time is allotted per class session?
   - How many class sessions do you teach?
   - Do you have any teaching assistants?

2. What are your students' initial skill levels?
   - Look for the rating charts located in the beginning of most steps or chapters to identify the criteria that discriminate between beginning, intermediate, and advanced skill levels.

3. What is the best order to teach golf skills?
   - Follow the sequence of steps (chapters) used in this book.
   - See Appendix C.1 for suggestions on when to introduce, review, or continue practicing each step.
   - Based on your answers to the previous questions, use the form in Appendix C.2 to order the steps that you will be able to cover in the time available.

4. What objectives do you want your students to accomplish by the end of a lesson, unit, or course?
   - For your technique or qualitative objectives, select from the Student Keys to Success (or the Keys to Success Checklists in *Golf: Steps to Success*) that are provided for all basic skills.

- For your performance or quantitative objectives, select from the Success Goals provided for each drill.
- For written questions on safety, rules, technique, tactics, history, and psychological aspects of golf, select from the various quizzes and the Test Bank of written questions.
- See the Sample Individual Program in Appendix D.1 for selected technique and performance objectives for a 16-week unit.
- For unit objectives, adjust your total number of selected objectives to fit your unit length (use the form in Appendix D.2).
- For organizing daily objectives, see the Sample Lesson Plan in Appendix E.1, and modify the basic lesson plan form in Appendix E.2 to best fit your needs.

5. How will you evaluate your students?

- Read the section on Evaluation Ideas. You may use the Putting Checklist in Appendix F. Because the Shotkeeper Scorecard is very helpful, you may want to reproduce it for your students' use. It can be found in Appendix G.
- Decide on your type of grading system, for example, letter grades, pass-fail, total points, percentages, skill levels (bronze, silver, gold), and so forth.

6. Which activities should be selected to achieve student objectives?

- Follow the drill and/or exercises for each step because they are specifically designed for large groups of students and are presented in a planned, easy-to-difficult order. Avoid a random approach to selecting drills and exercises.
- Modify drills as necessary to best fit your students' skill levels by following the suggestions for decreasing and increasing the difficulty level of each drill.
- Ask students to meet the Success Goal listed for each drill.
- Use the cross-reference to the corresponding step and drill number within the participants' book, *Golf: Steps to Success*, for class assignments or makeups.

7. What rules and expectations do you have for your class?

- For general management and safety guidelines, read the section "Preparing Your Class for Success."
- For specific guidelines, read the section "Group Management and Safety Tips" included with each drill.
- Let your students know what your rules are during your class orientation and/or first day of class. Then post them and repeat them often.

Teaching is a complex task, requiring you to make many decisions that will affect both you and your students (see Figure 1). Use this book to create an effective and successful learning experience for you and everyone you teach. And remember, have fun too!

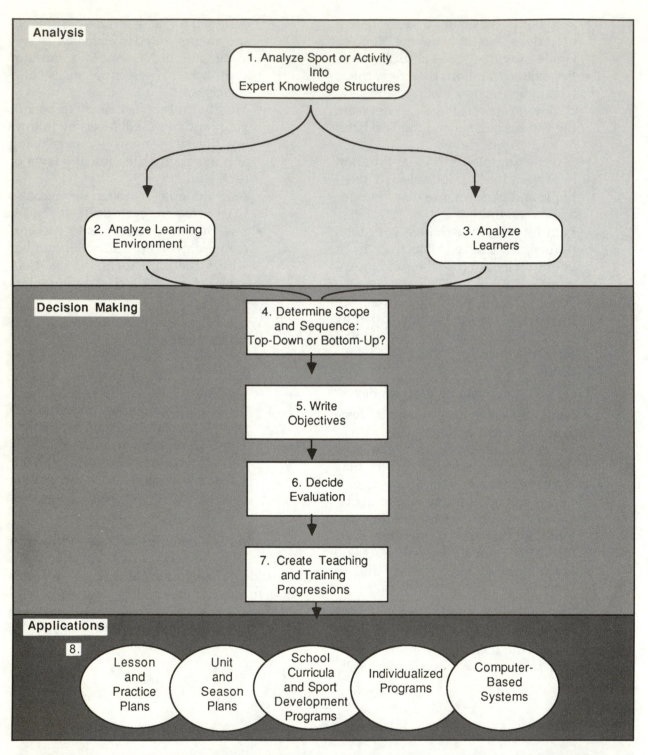

Note. From *Instructional Design for Teaching Physical Activities* by J.N. Vickers, in press, Champaign, IL: Human Kinetics. Copyright by Joan N. Vickers. Reprinted by permission. This instructional design model has appeared in earlier forms in *Badminton: A Structures of Knowledge Approach* (p. 1) by J.N. Vickers and D. Brecht, 1987, Calgary, AB: University Printing Services. Copyright 1987 by Joan N. Vickers; and ''The Role of Expert Knowledge Structures in an Instructional Design Model for Physical Education'' by J.N. Vickers, 1983, *Journal of Teaching in Physical Education*, **2**(3), p. 20. Copyright 1983 by Joan N. Vickers.

Preparing Your Class for Success

Before you begin teaching your class, you need to make many procedural decisions. Golf can be taught effectively indoors or outdoors. However, the two conditions create different learning environments that need to be considered in your planning. Specifically, when indoors you need to have a variety of activities and stations to maintain student interest and motivation to learn. More practice hitting is possible indoors because less time is consumed in retrieving balls. However, boredom can come quickly if other options are not planned.

Process teaching is highly effective indoors. Outdoors, student motivation is usually higher because the results of their efforts are more obvious and the learning effect from ball flight is quite high. The product orientation of the students as they focus on distance or accuracy may override your desires to teach through process to product. A blend of indoor and outdoor work is the most effective.

GENERAL CLASS MANAGEMENT

Safety in golf is critical. Clubs and golf balls can both be dangerous. It is therefore important to establish the first rule: No one swings a club or hits a ball after the signal. You may choose to use a whistle or a hand clap, but the signal must mean ''Stop!''—not ''You may hit just one more,'' but ''Stop right now!''

Rules of Golf Class

- Swing clubs only in designated areas.
- Never walk near swinging clubs.
- Swing clubs in one direction only.
- Whistle (signal) means STOP immediately.
- Pick up same number of balls as you hit.

It is also important to mark the appropriate hitting areas. Ropes or cones can be used to indicate the areas in which clubs may be swung. Within those appropriate areas, all clubs should be swung in the same direction, and left-handers should always be at the right end of a practice row (when looking toward the target area).

Retrieving golf balls that have been struck is also potentially dangerous, for two reasons: (a) students swinging clubs must completely stop before anyone moves outside the hitting zone toward the target areas; and (b) balls that are not picked up can be dangerous for participants in other sports (e.g., soccer on the same field, basketball players in the gym).

CLASS ORGANIZATION TECHNIQUES

In order to maximize student learning and maintain interest, use the following suggestions:

Class Organization Techniques

- Keep explanations short.
- Use Keys to Success.
- Provide goals and feedback for each segment.
- Use line formation outside.
- Use parallel lines formation inside.

When introducing new information, present only two or three key points at a time, then allow student practice. During practice, encourage students to take their time and learn to match the feel of each swing with the resultant ball flight. In golf the key is to develop good habits for alignment and setup and to learn from each swing.

IDEAS FOR TARGET UTILIZATION

Targets are important in establishing ''target awareness'' in all aspects of the game. They help to create a motivational and interesting learning environment for the students and yourself. A bare open field can easily be transformed into an area of targets varying in size, shape, and color that gets students excited and challenged when they come to class. Your gymnasium and field area have a wealth of potential targets. A few of these are listed below.

Gymnasium and Field Targets

jump ropes	hurdles
cones	hula hoops
bases	tables
flags	badminton nets
towels	volleyball nets
lime marks	archery targets
chairs	long jump pits
lacrosse goals	backstops
soccer goals	floor markings
basketball goals	tumbling mats
football goals	

The number of targets, particularly in the field area, will vary with the activity. Generally, there should be more targets at the shorter distances. This prevents students on the end of the lines from angling their alignment too sharply toward center targets, creating an unsafe situation. Figure 1 illustrates how targets can be used for the full swing, pitching, and chipping. Note specifically the recommendations for the number of students utilizing each target and the approximate distances.

CLASS WARM-UPS AND COOL-DOWNS

The warm-up drills for golf are designed primarily to increase circulation to enhance the effectiveness of the flexibility and strengthening exercises. Particular attention should be directed to stretching the lower back and shoulder muscles.

Students should do the prescribed exercises each time they intend to practice their golf skills (see ''Preparing Your Body for Success'' in *Golf: Steps to Success*). If your teaching style allows, provide an introduction of the routine

Full swing
3 students/target 50-79 yards
4 students/target 80-99 yards
5 students/target 100 or more yards

Pitching
2 students/target 20-49 yards
3 students/target 50-79 yards
4 students/target 80 or more yards

Chipping
4 students/target 5-14 yards
5 students/target 15-25 yards

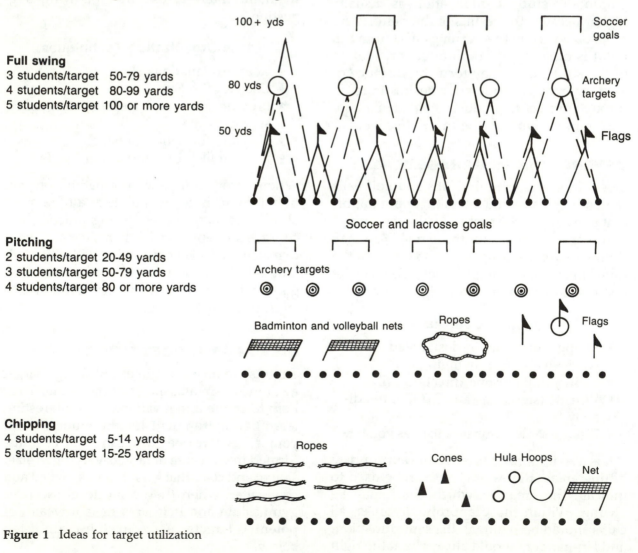

Figure 1 Ideas for target utilization

during the first class session. Then encourage students to warm up on their own before every class begins. This places responsibility on the students and should encourage warm-up outside of class. Otherwise, if you prefer to have a command-style class, you may wish to require simultaneous warm-ups by all students.

EQUIPMENT PREPARATION BEFORE CLASS

Before each class period all golf clubs should be checked for safety. The heads of the clubs must be secure and the shafts undented. A dented shaft is extremely weak and must not be used! Worn or smooth grips should be replaced.

The golf ball containers with plastic balls should also be checked to be sure that no hard balls were mistakenly placed in with the plastic balls. Using different colored balls would certainly make this an easier process, though students can also be assigned these checking tasks if they understand their importance. If hard and plastic balls are used in the same class session, place containers in opposite areas.

Preparing the teaching environment is also important. Be sure that designated "safe hitting areas" have been clearly marked before students arrive. You may also wish to place appropriate targets and practice areas into place before students arrive, or organize the students themselves to share in the responsibility for setting up and taking down equipment.

Equipment Preparation

- Check all clubs for loose heads, bent shafts, and worn grips.
- Keep plastic and hard balls separated.
- Establish "safe hitting areas."

SAFETY

Safety is a major consideration in golf instruction. Safety rules should be dated, distributed, and discussed with the class. Posting specific safety rules in the gymnasium, locker rooms, and the outdoor area can produce safety awareness in your students. Your personal attention to safety can be a strong influence and should be reflected in your safety rules posters.

Student Safety Rules

- Warm up before each class.
- Check clubs before swinging.
- Swing clubs only in "safe hitting areas."
- Stop all action on signal (whistle).
- Retrieve balls only when told to do so.
- Retrieve the same number of balls you hit.
- Keep hard and plastic balls separate.
- Everyone hits in same direction.
- Left-handers on right-end swing stations.

The following example of a golf safety poster can be easily created and posted around your gym and outside hitting areas (see Figure 2).

In order to make these rules meaningful, you must demonstrate your commitment to safety through your actions. The safe hitting areas should be clearly marked before students enter the learning area. In addition, there are other safety precautions you should take beyond those you expect of your students:

Instructor Safety Procedures

- Check all equipment before the unit begins.
- Mark "men's" and "women's" clubs.
- Have special clubs available (small and large grips).
- Store hard and plastic balls in separate, distinguishable containers.
- Have towels to dry hands.
- Pick up all tees (even broken ones) after each class.
- Post warning signs at edges of practice fields (or doors of gym) reading "Golf Class in Progress."
- Direct hitting away from crossings (indoors, away from doors).
- Distribute "Student Safety Rules" to students (written).
- Set targets in field so students on ends do not have to aim across the line of other students.

GOLF SAFETY

- Swing only in the designated areas
- Listen for signal
  — To hit
  — To retrieve
- Count your golf balls
- Pick up all golf balls

Figure 2 Golf Safety Poster

PRECLASS CHECKLIST

You may find it helpful to attach the following preclass checklist to your golf class roll or clipboard. Each item is important in conducting a safe and effective golf class.

1. Check ball buckets (plastic and hard balls).
2. Check equipment before class begins.
3. Review drills, noting equipment needs and progressions to use.
4. Have all needed equipment and checklists set out for the day.
5. Be sure there are towels available if the weather is hot.
6. Check the field area for use, posting safety rules.
7. Have rainy day plans ready for each class.
8. Have students count balls both before and after hitting them.

LEGAL DUTIES FOR GOLF

Eight legal duties are required of golf instructors to fulfill the obligations of liability. The following list is given to assist you in providing a safe and educationally sound golf program.

1. **Adequate Supervision**

   As an instructor, you must provide adequate supervision to protect students from inherent or extraneous hazards of the situation.

2. **Sound Planning**

   You must provide good, sound planning for the activities being conducted. Sound teaching progressions must be coupled with safe practice environments.

3. **Inherent Risks**

   We have outlined the inherent risks involved in golf. You have a duty to warn students adequately of such risks and to be sure they understand them. Emphasize safety whenever clubs are being swung.

4. Safe Environment

You must provide a practice area that is free of hidden or unmarked hazards. A safe environment includes the areas from which golf balls are hit and into which they may fly. You are expected to inspect the facility and equipment regularly and thoroughly and to pick up all balls and equipment daily.

5. Evaluating Students' Fitness for the Activity

You must evaluate any student injuries or handicaps and determine to what extent they may limit a student's safe participation. Checking for back, shoulder, and hip problems is especially important in golf. You must also attempt to ascertain the mental attitudes of students where such attitudes may become a hazard to their safety.

6. Emergency First Aid Procedures

The best way to deal with an accident is to prevent it. Keep hitting areas clearly marked, and direct students to pick up their balls simultaneously. If an accident does occur, you must be prepared to provide adequate medical assistance. It is your duty to your students to have planned and posted medical procedures that can be put into action immediately. Failure to provide this protection can result in a court finding of negligence.

7. Other Legal Concerns

You cannot restrict your classes or your students in any way that violates civil rights. Your legal duty is to provide for the legal rights and concerns of your students and staff and any spectators allowed during the program.

8. General Legal Concerns

In today's lawsuit-happy environment, you must be aware of all the possibilities for liability and take adequate measures to protect yourself. Always keep accurate records of your activities, especially in the event of an accident involving an injury. Keep such records for a minimum of 5 years. It is a wise practice for all instructors to carry adequate personal liability insurance. Rates for such insurance have risen dramatically in recent years, but the consequences of being uninsured could be quite serious.

The selection, purchase, and care of equipment is important in designing and implementing an effective golf unit. Many of the safety issues discussed in "Preparing Your Class for Success" are directly related to equipment.

WHY IS SELECTION OF EQUIPMENT IMPORTANT?

Golf equipment has changed over the years to the benefit of the player. Equipment is lighter overall, with more variability in lengths, grips, sizes, and lies. Now the learner can select equipment appropriate for his or her size and needs rather than try to fit the abilities and needs to the established, standard equipment. As an instructor, the availability of special equipment is exciting because it improves the potential for success of each of your students.

The type of equipment you purchase for use in your golf classes should result from your consideration of successful learning as the first priority. The second priority should be an awareness of students' future needs based on the skill they will develop through your class and beyond.

EQUIPMENT PREPARATION

Store the clubs to make them easily accessible and transportable, depending upon your facility. Separating the clubs by type—woods, 5-irons, 7- and 9-irons, pitching wedges (PW), sand wedges (SW), and putters—will make them readily available for their use in specific applications in each step. Old golf bags, baseball bat bags, or laundry bags make convenient storage containers for each type of club.

Your climatic conditions will determine your indoor or outdoor teaching needs. If your weather is unpredictable, it would be beneficial to prepare lesson plans for both because creating an effective indoor golf area in a gymnasium requires a greater variety of equipment and time in preparation.

EQUIPMENT NEEDS

Teaching golf requires some specific equipment designed only for golf—golf clubs, golf balls, tees—and a great deal of imagination in using other pieces of equipment often found in a gymnasium.

Golf Clubs and Balls

For a class of 20 students, you should have clubs that have composition rubber grips, preferably with finger markings (guides) permanently printed on them. Due to the potential for breaking or losing clubs, a minimum of 2 extras should be available for each specific club type. Therefore, the numbers to follow would be appropriate for coed classes of 20 students, or could be adjusted (increased or decreased) proportionally.

It is also recommended that half of the clubs be "men's" and half be "women's" (which are generally shorter and lighter than men's clubs). The labels *men's* and *women's* are standard in the industry, but for class purposes it is recommended that different colored tape be placed on them and that they be referred to by color rather than by sex. This makes it easier for the students to distinguish the clubs.

Equipment Needed

Woods

5-woods: 12 right-handed, 3 left-handed

7-woods: 12 right-handed, 3 left-handed
(A driver and a 3-wood will be needed for demonstration, but they can be borrowed or simulated without direct purchase)

Irons

5-irons: 22 right-handed, 3 left-handed

7-irons: 12 right-handed, 3 left-handed

9-irons: 12 right-handed, 3 left-handed

PW: 12 right-handed, 3 left-handed

SW: 12 right-handed, 3 left-handed

Putters: 12 right-handed, 3 left-handed

Preformed, Molded Grips on Irons

4 right-handed preformed grips should be placed on 5- or 7-irons

2 left-handed preformed grips should be placed on 5- or 7-irons

Golf Balls

Hard balls: 30 per student (plus 400 extra) (marked range balls are best to reduce theft)

Plastic balls: 20 per student (plus 100 extra)

Plastic containers or buckets for golf balls in 2 different colors to separate hard from plastic balls

Wooden Tees

40 per student (plastic tees are more expensive)

Brush Mats With Rubber Supports
(3 feet × 4 feet)

1 per student or 1 per 2 students (carpet squares 3 feet × 4 feet could be used, but smaller ones move too much and are not as safe)

Rubber Tees

3 per rubber mat

Putting Carpet Strips
(3 feet × 30 feet)

4 (one per 5 students)

Metal Putting Cups

8 (2 per putting strip)

Supplemental Equipment Used in Golf and Other Teaching Units

Towels: 1 per student

Cones: 20 small orange traffic cones

Target Flags: 20 (end line flags from field sports work well)

Jump Ropes: 25

Hula Hoops: 20

Golf Shafts: 10 (save broken club shafts)

Mirrors: 2 (door-size)

Badminton or Volleyball Nets and Standards: 4 sets

3-Foot Boards: 20 (made of two-by-fours)

Broom Handles: 10

Elastic Bands: 10 (2 inches × 36 inches)

Weighted Clubs: 5

Diagram of Golf Hole: 1 (large cloth diagram for teaching rules and etiquette)

Water-Based Paint: 3 spray cans (obtain permission from maintenance to use on the field)

Crepe Paper Streamers: 8 rolls

Videotape Equipment

Videotape Player and Monitor

Videotape Camera and Monitor

Blank Videotapes: 6

Instructional Videotapes (see Suggested References)

Sybervision
Golf Digest Instructional Tapes
National Golf Foundation Instructional Tapes
Crenshaw Putting Tape
Rules of Golf

MEETING INDIVIDUAL NEEDS OF STUDENTS WITH EQUIPMENT

A majority of your students will be able to use golf clubs that are standard-sized in terms of weight, length, lie, and grip size. However, there are also students who are at the extremes of the standard. These students will not meet with the same success unless it is planned for in the selection of equipment. For example, students who are exceptionally tall or short, or have relatively small or large hands, would find standard equipment a detriment to their learning.

In order to accommodate the needs of such special students, the following recommendations are provided:

1. Select majority of equipment based on standards for men and women.
2. Select special equipment for a minimum of 3 students (or 15% of class) at each of the "extremes"
   - shorter shafts with undersized grips
   - longer shafts with oversized grips
   - women's shafts with oversized grips
   - men's shafts with undersized grips

CHOOSING CLUBS FOR SUCCESSFUL LEARNING

Success in golf will initially be measured by your students in terms of getting the ball airborne. Therefore the clubs you use to teach various skills should have more loft and shorter, more manageable lengths, compared to accomplished players' needs. Based on this, the equipment list contains more lofted fairway woods and middle irons, rather than the longer drivers or long irons. Unfortunately, many classes were formerly taught with 1- and 3-woods and 3-irons, which are difficult to manage for beginners and even most higher skilled players. Instead, a combination of the 5- or 7-wood (with 7-woods preferable), 5-, 7-, and 9-irons, pitching wedges (PW), sand wedges (SW), and putters is recommended for most class purposes.

A full set of clubs should be available for purposes of illustration. These can usually be borrowed. In fact, the long irons and woods may be unsafe and inappropriate for practice facilities.

TEACHING AIDS

Golf instruction is greatly enhanced by the use of teaching aids. These aids can provide immediate feedback specific to swing needs and serve as additional ''teachers.'' Most aids are available for little or no expense, which makes their use more attractive! Students can also find ways to acquire similar aids for their own outside practice. For example, the following aids can be used for several purposes:

Teaching Aid	Use
3-foot boards (two-by-fours)	Alignment, weight distribution, ball placement, sand practice
Shafts	Alignment, ball position, swing center, angle of approach, path, plane, targets
Water-based paint	Alignment, ball position, path versus curve errors, safety markers, targets
Mirrors	Visual swing awareness and feel
Broom handles	Flexibility exercises, plane, alignment
Elastic straps	Arm swing
Jump ropes	Endurance training, alignment lines, path, targets, flexibility
Weighted clubs	Swing feel, conditioning
Molded grips	Grip position training
Hula hoops	Targets, safety markers

Teaching aids can also be constructed with little cost and effort. A list of these aids is provided in Appendix B with their purpose, the necessary materials, and the directions for their construction.

A teaching aid should be used for a specific purpose. The ones suggested have multiple uses. Be sure the student is given directions on *how* best to utilize the aid and on the *desired* outcome regarding feel and ball flight results.

ADAPTATION OF INDOOR FACILITIES

Indoor instruction is often a necessity and provides a good change of pace from outdoor practice. A gym can be transformed into an exciting and motivating area for golf. It takes preparation, but it can be fun and creative. Equipment such as the following is readily available in most gyms:

Badminton nets and standards

Basketball goals

Cones

Crepe paper streamers

Folding chairs

Hand dumbbells

Hula hoops

Masking tape

Mirror

Record player or cassette player

Ropes (long and short jump ropes)

Tumbling mats

Volleyball nets and standards

ORGANIZING INDOOR FACILITIES

Organizing your gymnasium into a variety of practice areas or stations can provide your students with a fun and effective learning experience. Depending on the amount of indoor time during a unit and the specific emphasis of instruction on a particular day, you can design the stations to meet your objectives. A timed rotation is encouragd to ensure that interest is maintained (see the Sample Facility Layout in Figure 3).

Each station should have a specific objective with success goals. The number of stations depends on the class objectives for the day, the number of students in your class, and the availability of equipment needed to meet the objectives. For example, if you have 20 students and the major objective for the class is introducing the full swing motion, there will be only minimal preparation of the facility. On the other hand, if you are reviewing the full swing motion and ball striking is an important facet of the lesson, but you have only 5 grass mats for 20 students, creativity is critical—or you should select an alternate objective for that session. Movies should be used sparingly and for specific purposes. Discussion before and after a movie is critical for an effective learning experience.

In organizing stations, remember to always hit in a direction away from the center, and avoiding doors or traffic patterns. Full swing stations should be set up a minimum of 8–10 yards from the wall, allowing space for the plastic balls to rebound. Establish safe hitting zones where students must not walk, due to swinging clubs. Review safety rules. Using cones or ropes to mark off safe hitting areas is very important. When setting mats, allow a minimum of 3 yards between each mat and at least 2 yards behind each.

Keys to Space Utilization

- Mats—3 yards minimum between, 2 yards minimum behind, 8 yards from wall for full swing
- Hitting Direction—toward outside walls
- Balls—hard and plastic balls in separate containers
- Markers—ropes or cones to separate stations

Sample Facility Layout

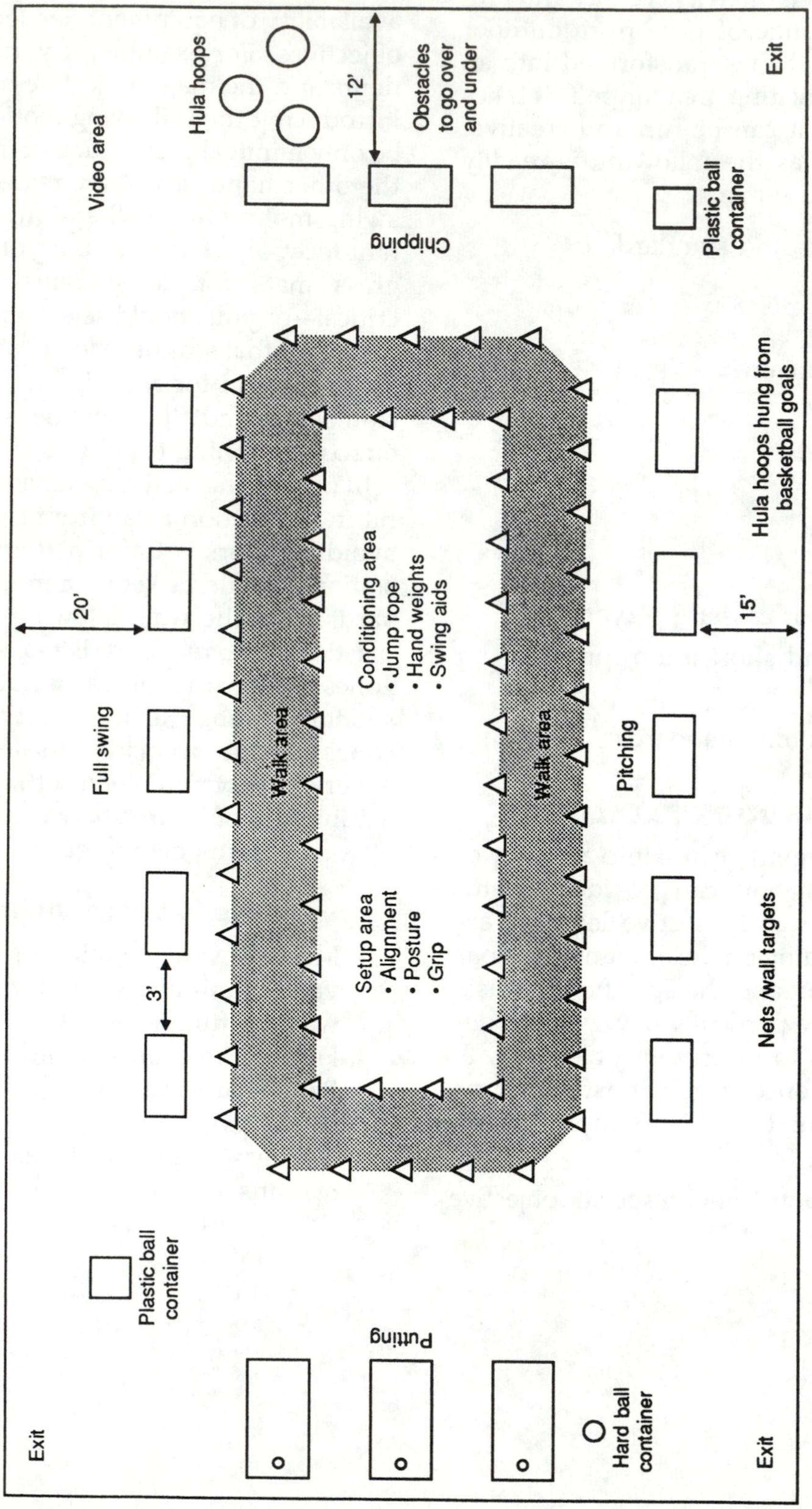

Figure 3 Facility Layout

Step 1   Experiencing the Full Swing Motion

The full swing motion of the golf swing is a complex motor skill, with 27 moving parts. However, by first introducing arm and body motion without the club, you can help your students develop the basic coordination of the swing without the intimidation of club and balls. Your emphasis should be on movement and freedom in swinging.

Your students will display a variety of skill levels in their general coordination of arms and body. This step and the next two are their foundation for building the swing. Developing a critical eye in this movement will help you in observing your students' performance here and in later steps. Many potential problems can be detected early through this observation. The criteria in the rating as well as the Keys to Success in the participant's book (see *Golf: Steps to Success*) can help you in your evaluation.

STUDENT KEYS TO SUCCESS

- Fluid motion
- Relaxed, free arm swing
- Whole body motion

Full Swing Rating

CRITERION	BEGINNING LEVEL	INTERMEDIATE LEVEL	ADVANCED LEVEL
Preparation Setup Posture	• Tends to sit back • Arms tense	• Sits back	• Over ball
Weight	• On heels	• On heels	• Midstep to balls of feet
Execution Backswing	• Restricted pivot • Lacks weight shift	• Freer pivot	• Consistent
Forwardswing	• Restricted pivot • Lacks weight shift • Overactive upper body	• Freer pivot	• Consistent
Follow-Through	• Balance inconsistent	• Balance consistent	• Balance consistent

Error Detection and Correction for the Full Swing Motion

Many of the errors in the full swing can be observed and corrected early through your students' practicing the full swing without a club and ball. The errors and corrections presented in the participant's book and below are common in beginning golfers. If you find one of these problems, refer to the right-hand side of the page to find out how to correct it. Select one error at a time to correct, in order to allow your students to focus on each important point of your teaching.

ERROR

CORRECTION

1. Thumbs point away from the target line on the backswing, resulting in too-active shoulders on forwardswing.

1. Student places a club on the ground under the arms at address, and parallel to the target line. Golfer practices swinging the arms on the club line back and through.

ERROR **CORRECTION**

2. Rear knee moves forward toward the target line on forwardswing, resulting in lack of weight shift and hip turn.

2. Have the student imagine cymbals on the knees to clang together on the backswing and the forwardswing.

3. Excessive knee flexion and increased angle at spine during address and set-up create tension and shift weight to heels.

3. Assign the Posture Club Drill (see *Golf*, Step 1, Drill 1) so student can feel spine angle with slight knee flexion, arms relaxing from shoulders, and weight forward midstep to balls of feet.

ERROR 🚫

CORRECTION

4. Arms move toward target line on backswing, decreasing body turn.

🚫

4a. Have student place club on ground (as in Correction 1) and practice swinging the arms back and through over the club.

   b. Assign Body Rotation Drill (see *Golf*, Step 1, Drill 2).

5. Upper body turns faster than lower body moves on backswing and forward-swing.

5. Assign Body Rotation Drill (see *Golf*, Step 1, Drill 2) and Elephant Trunk Drill (see *Golf*, Step 1, Drill 3).

Selected Full Swing Motion Drills

1. *Posture Drill*
[Corresponds to *Golf*, Step 1, Drill 1]

Group Management and Safety Tips

- All students can practice at one time.
- Use parallel line formation (two lines facing each other) to facilitate viewing of all students and making corrections. Otherwise line up students with left-handers at the right end of the line (for future steps).
- Partner work is effective.

Equipment

- Golf clubs, 1 per student (or 1 wand or shaft per student)

Instructions to Class

- ''Rehearse the proper posture, feeling as though you are in a 'ready' position.''
- ''Remember—if the club comes off your back, you have bent too far over.''
- ''With proper position you should be able to tap your heels, feeling the weight on your feet over the midstep to the balls of your feet.''

Student Options

- ''After 5 repetitions, work with a partner, alternating between taking posture with and without the club down your back.''
- ''Have partner evaluate posture.''

Student Success Goal

- 10 repetitions with club down back and correct posture

To Reduce Difficulty

- Not applicable

To Increase Difficulty

- Have student practice with eyes closed.

2. Body Rotation Drill
[Corresponds to *Golf*, Step 1, Drill 2]

Group Management and Safety Tips

- All students can practice at once.
- Use semicircle formation, students arm's length apart, and target shoulders toward inside.
- Be sure students are shifting weight to reduce back tension.
- Movement should be *smooth and slow*, not fast.

Equipment

- Golf clubs, 1 per student

Instructions to Class

- "Imagine your target is to the inside of the circle."
- "As you practice the turn, you will feel the muscles in your back on the target side stretch on the backswing, and those on the rear side stretch on the forwardswing."
- "Hold the backswing and forwardswing momentarily on the first 4 turns, in order to feel the stretch."
- "The turn is smooth and continuous, with no up-and-down movement."

Student Option

- "Work with a partner, holding the head from in front during the body rotation."

Student Success Goal

- 15 total rotations

    5 rotations with eyes open

    5 rotations with eyes closed

    5 rotations with eyes open

To Reduce Difficulty

- Have student stand erect, extending both arms horizontally to form a straight line across the shoulders. Golfer takes proper position and practices the turn, maintaining both arms extended while turning. At end of backswing, the target arm is straight in front of the body, over the imaginary ball. The arms indicate the amount and angle of the shoulder turn.

To Increase Difficulty

- Increase the required number of repetitions to 20.

3. Elephant Trunk Swing Drill or Pendulum Swing
[Corresponds to *Golf*, Step 1, Drill 3]

Group Management and Safety Tips
- All students can practice at once.
- Students take semicircle formation with rear shoulders toward the center (as if hitting out, away from the center).

Equipment
- None

Instructions to Class
- "Your arms and shoulders should be free of tension as you take your posture."
- "The arms swing freely *from* the shoulders, not *by* the shoulders."
- "Your arms should move from the shoulder joint in a manner similar to the way that you move your lower arm from the elbow joint without moving your upper arm."
- "Stand erect. Let your arms relax."
- "Swing your arms back and forth as if you were marching."
- "Note how your shoulders are not moving forward at the same time as your arms."
- "This is how your arms swing *from* your shoulders."
- "Now let's try moving your shoulders forward at the same time as your arms."
- "Not so easy. The movement of the arms is stifled."
- "Take your posture and practice feeling your arms move *from* your shoulders."

- "As your arms begin to swing past your legs and up, allow your body to respond to the swinging motion."
- "Allow your body to turn around an imaginary center point."
- "Feel your weight shift to the rear side by turning your target knee into the rear knee allowing your target heel to raise slightly off the ground."
- "Feel your weight shift back to the target side by returning your target heel to the ground and turning your rear knee into your target knee."
- "Create a lot of motion."

Student Option
- "Work with a partner observing."

Student Success Goal
- 10 swings with correct form

To Reduce Difficulty
- Have student practice half-swings with arms parallel to the ground during backswing and forwardswing.

To Increase Difficulty
- Have student grip a golf club in middle of shaft, the target hand with palm down and rear palm facing up. Student should swing using the elephant guidelines.
- Golfer could practice with eyes closed.

4. Arm Swing and Turn Drill
[Corresponds to *Golf*, Step 1, Drill 4]

Group Management and Safety Tips

- All students can practice at once.
- This is partner work in a semicircle.

Equipment

- None

Instructions to Class

- "As you work with your partners, let your hand on their head be a *reminder* to feel the turning motion around a center."
- "Your head moves a few inches horizontally during the swing; it is not completely stationary."
- "Avoid vertical movement of your body during the swing."

Student Option

- "Practice with a partner or keep head steady on a wall while the body turns."

Student Success Goal

- 10 repetitions feeling turn around a fixed center

To Reduce Difficulty

- Have partner place hands a few inches away from the sides of the golfer's head, allowing some room for head movement.

To Increase Difficulty

- Have student practice with eyes closed.
- Partner holds finger just off the center of swinger's head to give no feedback to swinger. After the swing, the swinger relates the amount of head movement felt.

5. Wheel Image Drill
[Corresponds to *Golf*, Step 1, Drill 5]

Group Management and Safety Tips

- All students can practice at once.

Equipment

- None

Instructions to Class

- "The golf swing can be pictured as a clock, with your head being the center of the clock. Imagine that your hands are the hands on the clock. With your hands pointing straight down, at 6 o'clock, call that *position 0*."
- "As your hands move back or forward one number to 7 o'clock or 5 o'clock, it is a *1* on either side of the 0 position."
- "Moving from 0 to the next spot (8 o'clock) would be a 2 backswing, with a matching 2 forwardswing up to the 4 o'clock position. Swinging to the clock's regular 9 o'clock and 3 o'clock positions can be labeled *3 swing lengths*, whereas 10 and 2 o'clock are 4 lengths, and 11 and 1 o'clock are 5 lengths."

Student Options

- "Watch films or videotapes of golfers swinging; visualize the players turning on a rod or the hub of a wheel."
- "Practice in front of a mirror that has horizontal and vertical lines taped on it."

Student Success Goal

- 10 repetitions with the correct form

To Reduce Difficulty

- Model the turn yourself, using a club down your back.
- Show illustrations of a wheel superimposed on golf swings.

To Increase Difficulty

- Have student practice with eyes closed.

Step 2 Setup

The importance of a consistent setup should not be overlooked in your teaching. As you observe your students, their setups will range from very methodical to "quick to hit." The amount of time in preparation is not the key element, but the consistency and effectiveness of the setup for each individual is critical. Always have your students begin practice sessions with alignment clubs, and alternate practice with and without their aid. Targets placed in the hitting area are also essential for developing consistent setups and target awareness.

STUDENT KEYS TO SUCCESS

- Consistency
- Reproducible grip
- Smoothness in routine

Setup Rating

CRITERION	BEGINNING LEVEL	INTERMEDIATE LEVEL	ADVANCED LEVEL
Grip	• Varies (rear hand under) • Tight pressure	• More consistent • Tight pressure	• Consistent • Light pressure
Posture	• Sits back on heels • Distance from ball varies	• Sits back • Too far away from ball	• Over ball • Consistent distance from ball
Ball Position	• Varies	• Too far forward	• Consistent
Alignment	• Closed or erratic	• More consistent (closed bias)	• Consistent

Error Detection and Correction for Setup

Full swing errors are often a result of an improper setup position. Time spent in developing the setup helps reduce future poor habits. Always check for errors in the setup position *first* (i.e., grip, alignment, and posture), followed by the backswing and forwardswing.

ERROR 🚫

CORRECTION

1. Target and rear hands too far under the club, in opposite directions with the club gripped more in the palms of both hands rather than in the fingers.

1. Have student establish a routine for gripping the club target hand first, then rear hand. Note checkpoints: grip diagonally across target hand palm to fingers, grip in rear hand fingers, and Vs to rear side of chin.

ERROR

CORRECTION

2. In the address position, the hands are behind the ball, establishing a *weak* target side and strong rear side on the backswing.

2. At address the club should feel like an extension of the target arm, with a straight line from the target shoulder through the club.

3. Arm position at address is too close to the body. Plumb line from the eyes would fall on the shaft.

3. Student should practice taking the posture without a club, noting where the arms hang from the shoulders. Then have student take the setup with the club, then open the hands, allowing the club to drop. The arms should remain in the same position.

4. Closed alignment of feet with square shoulders and blade to target create an outside-in club path, due to arms being too close at address (causing a pulled shot).

4. Recommend using a club or two-by-four for alignment practice, and developing a setup routine (see *Golf*, Step 2).

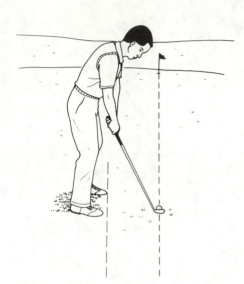

5. Swing center is behind the ball at address with the irons, tending to cause thin or fat shots.

5. Place a shaft in the ground in line with the ball. The golfer's swing center should be over, or slightly in front of, the ball at address.

ERROR   **CORRECTION**

6. Rear arm is extended and tight, causing the rear shoulder to be tense. This forces open shoulders, resulting in an outside-in swing path; high, weak shots; and a pull or slice.

6. Have student allow the rear arm and shoulder to be more relaxed at setup. When standing on rear side of golfer, you should be able to see the target arm.

7. Target arm is extended and tight, causing the target shoulder to be tense. This forces the shoulders closed, resulting in an inside-out swing and push or hook shots.

7. Tell student to allow target arm and target shoulder to be more relaxed. You should see no space between the target and rear arm from the rear side (see Correction 6).

ERROR 🚫

CORRECTION

8. Target hand grip is more in the palm, reducing club head speed, and the club appearing as though it extends up the arms.

8. Have golfer practice the Grip Drill (Drill 1); the club should appear to point toward the belt buckle.

Selected Setup Drills

1. Grip Drill

[Corresponds to *Golf*, Step 2, Drill 1]

Group Management and Safety Tips

- For safety, allow *no swinging* of clubs at this time.
- All students may practice at one time, allowing for equipment.
- Partner work is effective.
- Arrange students in semicircle formation (5 feet between students) to facilitate observations and corrections.

Equipment

- Golf clubs, 1 per student (5-, 7-, or 9-iron, 5- or 7-wood)
- Molded form grips on a few demonstration clubs

Instructions to Class

- "As you practice taking your grip, establish a routine to use *each and every time*."
- "Always place your *target* hand on the club first, then your rear hand."
- "Hold the club as *lightly as you can without letting it flop in your hands*."

Student Options

- "Practice with a partner checking the correctness of your grip using the checklist."
- "Alternate taking grip with a wood, then an iron."

Student Success Goal

- 10 repetitions in a row with all checkpoints correct

To Reduce Difficulty

- Have student do 5 repetitions with a partner reading out checkpoints.
- Student could do 5 repetitions with eyes open, then 5 with eyes closed.
- Draw lines on student's hands with washable ink; have student match up the lines for each hand.
- Have student alternate between molded grip and regular grip.

To Increase Difficulty

- Have student alternate taking various grip positions, and have a partner check for correctness or make adjustments.
- Recommend practicing taking different grip pressures and noting the change in feel using

  tight target hand, light rear hand

  light target hand, tight rear hand

  tight target and rear hands

  light target and rear hands

2. Weight Distribution Drill
[Corresponds to *Golf*, Step 2, Drill 2]

Group Management and Safety Tips

- For safety, allow *no swinging* of clubs at this point.
- All students can practice at one time, allowing for equipment.
- Use a line formation, with 6 feet between students, to facilitate corrections.
- Partner work is effective.

Equipment

- Golf clubs, 1 per student (5-, 7-, 9-irons, 5-, 7-wood)
- Molded form grip clubs
- Two-by-fours or shafts for alignment
- Golf balls, 1 per student

Instruction to Class

- ''Between each repetition, practice taking your setup position using the suggested routine.''

Student Options

- ''Work with a partner, using the setup checklist.''
- ''Practice each of the setup positions with your eyes open, then closed. Are you more aware of the differences in the weight distribution with your eyes open, or closed?''

Student Success Goal

- 9 total setups, alternating the stance

  3 setup positions forward

  3 setup positions backward

  3 setup positions balanced

To Reduce Difficulty

- Have student practice taking only the proper stance.
- Golfer may alternate between the proper stance and either the backward or forward position.
- Have student practice with a two-by-four, taking setup with heels on the board, toes on the board, and without board with weight midstep to balls of the feet.

To Increase Difficulty

- Suggest practicing with eyes closed.

3. *Walk Away Alignment Drill*
[Corresponds to *Golf*, Step 2, Drill 3]

Group Management and Safety Tips

- For safety, allow *no swinging* of clubs.
- All students can practice at one time, allowing for equipment.
- Partner work is effective.
- Use line formation initially to enhance corrections; then students can scatter for partner and individual practice.

Equipment

- Golf clubs, 1 per student (5-, 7-, 9-iron, 5-, 7-wood)
- Tees, 1 per student
- Golf balls, 1 per student

Instructions to Class

- ''Use a tee as your imaginary target for the first 3 repetitions.''
- ''Place the tee no more than 6–8 inches from the ball.''
- ''Be precise.''
- ''Use the suggested routine: grip, club alignment, posture, stance.''

Student Options

- ''Work with a partner, changing targets and going through the routine.''
- ''With a partner, play a game of Bogey, getting a letter for each misalignment like Horse in basketball.''

Student Success Goal

- 10 repetitions in a row with correct alignment

To Reduce Difficulty

- Reduce Success Goal to 7 repetitions.
- Place an alignment club on the ground for student to practice taking setup.
- Have golfer alternate between using the alignment club and not.
- Place a tee in front of the ball as an alignment guide for student to practice the alignment drill.

To Increase Difficulty

- Golfer can work with a partner on an accuracy of alignment contest.
- Expand the Success Goal to include alignment accuracy and meeting all items on Setup Checklist 7 of 10 times.

4. Arm Hang Drill
[Corresponds to *Golf*, Step 2, Drill 4]

Group Management and Safety Tips

- For safety, allow *no swinging* of golf clubs.
- All students can practice at one time, depending on equipment.
- Partner work is effective.
- Use a parallel line formation (6 feet between students) initially, to facilitate corrections.

Equipment

- Golf clubs, 1 per student (5-, 7-, 9-irons, 5-, 7-woods)
- Golf balls, 1 per student

Instructions to Class

- "You want to feel that your arms are relaxed and hanging free."
- "Lightness in your grip pressure and arms helps you create a faster arm swing, making for greater shot distance. This begins in your setup."

Student Options

- "Alternate with a wood and an iron. Do you feel a difference in the setup?"
- "With a partner looking on, alternate with a wood and iron. Have the partner use the checklist, noting (a) consistency in the setup when switching clubs and (b) areas that tend to be less consistent."

Student Success Goal

- 10 repetitions with correct distance from the ball determined by the arms resuming a relaxed position when the club is released

To Reduce Difficulty

- Permit use of only the 9- and 7-irons.

To Increase Difficulty

- Expand Success Goal to include correct grip, as well as correct relationship to ball, in the 10 repetitions.

5. *Setup Sequence Drill*
[Corresponds to *Golf*, Step 2, Drill 5]

Group Management and Safety Tips

- For safety, allow *no swinging* of clubs.
- All students can practice at one time.
- Use line formation (at least 3 yards between each station), all golfers with target shoulders toward targets.
- Partner work is effective.
- Initially, for the first 3 repetitions, have all students walk through the sequence in unison, as you verbalize the sequence.

Equipment

- Golf clubs, 1 per student (5-, 7-, 9-irons, 5-, 7-woods)
- Balls, 1 per student
- 12 targets set in 4 rows, 3 per distances at 30, 50, 70, and 90 yards

Instructions to Class

- "As you practice and play, always have a specific target. Practice your setup in relation to the target."
- "Initially use the following sequence to develop a feel for a consistent procedure." [*Note*: Demonstrate this sequence yourself, verbalizing each step.]

  "Select your target from behind the ball."

  "Find an intermediate target spot."

  "Select a club."

  "Grip your club from behind the ball."

  "Walk up to the ball."

  "Set the club alignment in relation to the intermediate target."

  "Set your posture."

  "Set your body alignment, setting one foot at a time, target foot first."

- "Alternate shooting at targets to the right and left at 30 and 50 yards."

Student Options

- "After 5 repetitions, alternate between taking grip behind the ball and taking grip on the side of the ball."
- "With a partner watching, after 5 repetitions alternate between taking grip behind the ball and taking grip on the side of the ball. Your partner, using the Setup Checklist, determines which procedure is the most accurate."
- "Alternate using woods and irons."

Student Success Goal

- 10 repetitions in exact sequence

To Reduce Difficulty

- Reduce repetitions required to 5.
- Student may use only irons.
- Shorten sequence to include only the aspects from behind the ball through clubface alignment.

To Increase Difficulty

- Expand Success Goal to include accurate clubface alignment.
- Expand Success Goal to include accuracy in both clubface *and* body alignment.

Step 3 Applying the Full Swing With Irons and Woods

Your beginning class will demonstrate a wide range of skill levels from student to student as well as from day to day. Your students may look like pros on their practice swings—but like beginners when actually striking the ball. This is not unusual. The ball initially creates tremendous intimidation. Recognize this and tell your students it is instinctive to try to make the ball go a long way. The drills are designed to help the students discover this. Be patient.

Stress the feel of a swinging motion (Step 1) as the clubs are introduced. Students often tend to revert from the free swinging motion they demonstrate without the club (Step 1) and in their practice swings to a ''hit impulse'' or become ''ball-bound.'' The hit impulse and ball-boundness occur when the student focuses on contacting the ball. The hit impulse is a fast, jerky upper body movement on the forward-swing, usually in an effort to create power to hit the ball a long way. Students who become ball-bound tend to restrict movement and appear stiff. Their swings are usually short and tend to decelerate coming into the ball to ensure contact. There is a fear of missing the ball. The full swing technique and the drills in this step will help to reduce these tendencies. Constant attention to the setup (Step 2) and target awareness will result in well-controlled and long shots, if technique and motion are stressed during practice and through your observations. The criteria in the rating and the Keys to Success (see *Golf: Steps to Success*) provide guidelines for your observations.

STUDENT KEYS TO SUCCESS

- Fluid motion
- Smooth, continuous flow of movement
- ''Quiet'' change of direction from backswing to forwardswing

Full Swing With Irons and Woods Rating

CRITERION	BEGINNING LEVEL	INTERMEDIATE LEVEL	ADVANCED LEVEL
Preparation **Setup** Alignment	• Inconsistent • Closed or erratic	• More consistent • More consistent (closed bias)	• Very consistent • Square
Ball Position	• Varies	• Ball placement more consistent	• Consistent placement
Grip	• Varies (rear hand under) • Tight pressure	• More consistent • Tight	• Consistent grip • Light
Execution **Backswing**	• Inconsistent length • Target arm bends • Restricted pivot • "Ball-bound"	• Consistent arc • Tends to restrict pivot • Begins target awareness	• Consistent arc • Full pivot • Target awareness
Forwardswing	• Erratic pace • Deceleration on forwardswing • Inconsistent release	• More consistent pace • Constant pace • More consistent release	• Constant acceleration • Varies pace by situation • Timed release
Follow-Through	• Lacks balance	• Consistent balance	• Balanced

Error Detection and Correction for Full Swing With Irons and Woods

Full swing errors can be detected from understanding the ball flight laws as presented in the participant's book (especially in Step 4) and through observing techniques described below. Both are important for you to know and utilize as a teacher.

ERROR

CORRECTION

1. There is a high, weak trajectory, pull-slice, or low pull with little distance, due to tight grip and tension in upper body, which creates an outside-in swing path on the forwardswing, with the upper body moving first and no weight shift.

1a. Check grip pressure (should be light) and recommend that the student practice the Cocking Drill (Drill 4) to feel the desired wrist action.

b. Recommend Weight Distribution Drill (see *Golf*, Step 2, Drill 2).

2. There are fat or thin shots due to weight shifting to target side during backswing and rear side on forward-swing (*reverse weight shift*).

2. Have golfer practice the proper weight shift by swinging the club back and raising the target foot off the ground; then swinging forward, stepping onto the target foot, and raising the rear foot off the ground. Student should feel the knee-to-knee touch with the heels off the ground while swinging.

3. There are fat or thin shots due to target arm collapsing on backswing.

3. Recommend Practice the Wide Whoosher Drill (Drill 1) for student to feel the target arm extension on the backswing and forwardswing.

4. There are thin or pulled shots due to weight staying on rear side during the forwardswing.

4. Golfer should practice having the target knee touch the rear knee on backswing, and rear knee touch target knee on forwardswing. Then student can move on to the full swing with ball.

ERROR

CORRECTION

5. There are thin or fat shots due to target shoulder tilting toward the ball on backswing, and the rear shoulder tilting toward the ball on the forward-swing.

5a. Recommend the Body Rotation Drill (Step 1, Drill 2), which emphasizes the contrasting feel in a shoulder tilt and desired turn.

b. Have student practice the Wide Whoosher Drill (Drill 1). Then use the desired turn while hitting balls.

6. There are pulled shots due to upper body starting the forwardswing before completion of the backswing.

6a. Have golfer practice making full backswings (swing length 5), pausing to feel the position and weight shift, then feeling the weight shift on forwardswing with the arm swing starting down.

b. Suggest word cues "back and through" for full backswing and hitting through the ball on forwardswing.

ERROR

CORRECTION

7. There are thin, fat, or weak shots due to wrist uncocking too soon from the top of swing (*casting*, the loss of arm and club angle).

7a. Have student practice 4-to-4 swing length, focusing on feeling the angle of club and wrist maintained past hip height, on the forwardswing before ball contact.

b. Recommend practicing the Cocking Drills (Drills 4 and 5) 3 times, then trying a full swing 3 times. Student should repeat 3 times, then alternate the Full Swing and Cocking Drills.

c. Student should focus on the arms starting the forwardswing, *with* the weight shift.

8. There are pushed or pulled shots due to low or flat backswing, resulting in lower body moving faster than the upper body on the forwardswing.

8a. Recommend the One-Leg Toe Drill (Drill 7); student should focus on the arm swing and wrist cocking, and maintaining balance.

b. Have golfer practice the swing path by placing a club on ground about 3 feet from the hip. With the 3-to-3 swing length, the arms should be on the target line side of the shaft, with the toe of the club pointing up.

Selected Full Swing With Irons and Woods Drills

1. Wide Whoosher Drill
[Corresponds to *Golf*, Step 3, Drill 1]

Group Management and Safety Tips

- Review safety procedures.
- Emphasize always swinging in the direction of open space.
- All students can practice at one time, allowing for equipment and space.
- Use a parallel line formation with rear shoulders toward the inside of the line, a minimum of 3 yards between students, and 6 yards between lines.
- Partner work is effective.

Equipment

- Golf clubs, 1 per student

Instructions to Class

- "The 'whooshing' should be heard as club comes down just past hip height and through the ball position."
- "Feel your thumbs point to the rear on the backswing, and down and to the target on the forwardswing."
- "Practice 3 swings at 50% speed first to feel the motion of the target arm with the weight shift."
- "Use a full body turn on the backswing and forwardswing."

Student Options

- "Practice with a partner; hold your club on the swinging partner's head to feel the turn about a center."
- "After 5 repetitions, alternate a regular full swing between each wide whoosher swing."

Student Success Goal

- 10 swings with a loud "whooshing" sound

To Reduce Difficulty

- Reduce repetitions required to 6.

To Increase Difficulty

- Increase repetitions required to 20.
- Have student swing with the target arm only, placing the rear hand on the back of the hip and pushing forward with it on the start of the forwardswing, in order to feel hip turn.

2. *Wheel Drill*
Without a Ball
[Corresponds to *Golf*, Step 3, Drill 2]

Group Management and Safety Tips

- Review safety procedures.
- Use a line formation with minimum of 3 yards between each student.
- All students face and swing in the same direction (*always put left-handers at right end of line*).
- Partner work is effective.

Equipment

- Golf clubs, minimum of 1 per student
- Checklist forms for full swing

Instructions to Class

- "Learning to *feel* and *control* the swing length of your forwardswing helps you develop a more consistent, repeatable swing and enhances your distance control."
- "Rehearse each phase of the swing, feeling the swing length and pace. Verbalize the swing length as you rehearse."

Student Options

- "Experiment with a variety of club lengths; note any differences in feel as you change lengths and clubs."
- "With a partner, use the checklist to evaluate technique."

Student Success Goal

- 20 total swings
  a. 10 total swings with a 5- or 7-iron
     2 swings, 1-to-1 swing length
     2 swings, 2-to-2 swing length
     2 swings, 3-to-3 swing length
     2 swings, 4-to-4 swing length
     2 swings, 5-to-5 swing length
  b. 10 total swings repeating (a), but with *eyes closed*

To Reduce Difficulty

- Make student practice only 3-to-3 and 5-to-5 swing lengths.
- Allow golfer to practice with eyes open only.

To Increase Difficulty

- Have student practice alternating swing lengths as follows, with eyes open: 5-to-5, 2-to-2, 4-to-4, 3-to-3, 1-to-1.
- Recommend practicing with a partner. Have nonswinging partner call out desired swing lengths. The swinging partner performs with eyes closed. At end of swing, partner provides feedback as to whether the swing length was correct and of equal length on backswing and forwardswing. If not, student must take an extra practice swing.

3. *Wheel Drill With a Ball*
[Corresponds to *Golf*, Step 3, Drill 3]

Group Management and Safety Tips

- Review safety rules for hitting and retrieving balls.
- All students may practice at one time, allowing for equipment and space.
- Line up students to swing and hit in the same direction.
- Be sure practice space is appropriate for potential club distances.
- Have 3 yards minimum between hitting stations (between each student).
- Left-handers stand at right end of line.
- Partner work is effective.

Equipment

- Golf clubs, minimum 1 per student (7- and 9-irons; extra 5-irons, 5- and 7-woods if possible)
- Golf balls, 25 per student or pair of students
- Tees, minimum of 6 per student
- Targets in the field, minimum of 6 placed at 50, 75, 100, 125, 150, and 175 yards

Instructions to the Class

- ''Rehearse each phase of the swing, feeling the swing lengths and swing pace.''
- ''Make 2 practice swings between each ball hit.''

Student Options

- ''Experiment with the 9- and 7-irons and swing lengths with a partner, comparing distances the ball travels with each club and/or swing length. Do any combinations produce similar results?''
- ''With a partner, use the checklist for technique evaluation.''

Student Success Goal

- 50 total swings
  - a. 25 swings with a ball elevated on a tee
    - 5 swings, 1-to-1 swing length
    - 5 swings, 2-to-2 swing length
    - 5 swings, 3-to-3 swing length
    - 5 swings, 4-to-4 swing length
    - 5 swings, 5-to-5 swing length
  - b. 25 swings with a ball resting on the ground (no tee)
    - 5 swings, 1-to-1 swing length
    - 5 swings, 2-to-2 swing length
    - 5 swings, 3-to-3 swing length
    - 5 swings, 4-to-4 swing length
    - 5 swings, 5-to-5 swing length

To Reduce Difficulty

- Make golfer practice only 3-to-3 and 5-to-5 swing lengths.
- Reduce repetitions required to 10, 2 in each situation.

To Increase Difficulty

- Make student practice with a 5-iron and 5- or 7-woods.
- Expand Success Goal to include accuracy within 15 yards right or left of a selected target.

4. Cocking Drill Without a Ball

[Corresponds with *Golf*, Step 3, Drill 4]

Group Management and Safety Tips

- Review safety procedures.
- All students can practice at one time, allowing for equipment and space.
- Use a line formation with students swinging and hitting into a field.
- Have 3 yards between each swing station or student.
- Ask if a student has back problems, if so, substitute One-Leg Toe Drill (Drill 7).
- Be sure practice space is appropriate for potential shot distances.

Equipment

- Golf clubs, 1 per student

Instructions to Class

- "Proper wrist action is necessary for distance and direction. Your grip pressure should be light, but not loose, to allow for wrist mobility."
- "Hold the backswing and forwardswing of the first 3 swings of each situation to feel the cocking and recocking of the wrists."

Student Options

- "After 5 repetitions of each situation, work with a partner. Observe your partner's wrist action, then visualize your own wrist action and arm swing, then adding the lower body."
- "After 5 repetitions of each situation, alternate (a), (b), and (c) in any order."

Student Success Goal

- 30 total swings using swing cue word each time
    a. 10 swings cocking, uncocking, and recocking wrists without moving arms
    b. 10 swings cocking, uncocking, and recocking wrists, with arms moving 3-to-3 swing length
    c. 10 swings cocking, uncocking, and recocking wrists, using arms and lower body motion

To Reduce Difficulty

- Have student practice only parts (a) and (c).
- Decrease total repetitions required to 18 or 12, 6 or 4 in each situation.

To Increase Difficulty

- Make student practice with a 5-iron and/or 7-wood.
- Recommend practicing with eyes closed.

5. Cocking Drill With a Ball
[Corresponds to *Golf*, Step 3, Drill 5]

Group Management and Safety Tips

- Review safety rules for hitting and retrieving balls.
- All students can practice at one time, allowing for equipment and space.
- Use a line formation with students swinging and hitting into a field.
- Have 3 yards between each swing station or student.
- Check for student who has back problems; substitute One-Leg Toe Drill (Drill 7).
- Be sure practice space is appropriate for potential shot distances.

Equipment

- Golf clubs, minimum of 1 per student (7- and 9-irons, with extra 7-woods and 5-irons)
- Golf balls, 25 per student
- Tees, minimum 6 per student
- Targets, 6 minimum; 10 needed to increase difficulty

Instructions to Class

- ''The wrist action of the cocking drill provides both distance and direction to the swing.''
- ''Hold the backswing and forwardswing of the first 3 swings to feel the cocking and recocking of the wrists.''
- ''Note the differences in the shot distance between using only the wrists and using the body with the wrists.''

Student Options

- ''Experiment with a variety of lofts, noting differences in feel and distance.''
- ''Work with a partner and checklist, reviewing setup as you practice.''

Student Success Goal

- 20 total swings using a word cue

    5 swings with ball on tee

    5 swings with ball not on tee

    5 more swings with ball on tee

    5 swings with ball not on tee

To Reduce Difficulty

- Have student practice with balls on tees only.
- Reduce repetitions required to 12 total swings, 3 in each condition.

To Increase Difficulty

- Have student hit without a tee.
- Make golfer practice with 5-iron and/or 7-wood.
- Expand Success Goal to include an accuracy element—the ball landing within 15 yards to the right or left of a designated target, for instance.

6. Distance Drill

[Corresponds to *Golf*, Step 3, Drill 6]

Group Management and Safety Tips

- Review safety rules for hitting and retrieving balls.
- All students can practice at one time, allowing for equipment and space.
- Use a line formation with students swinging and hitting into a field.
- Have a minimum of 3 yards between each swing station or student.
- Check for student who has back problems; substitute One-Leg Toe Drill (Drill 7).
- Be sure space is appropriate for potential shot distances.

Equipment

- Golf clubs (a wood and iron per student, e.g., 5-, 7-, 9-irons, 3-, 5-, and 7-woods)
- Golf balls, 25 per student
- Tees, minimum 6 per student
- Targets set at 10-yard intervals, 60–160 yards
- Recording sheets (see *Golf*, Step 3, Drill 5, Your Score)

Instructions to Class

- ''The objective is to combine control of distance with control of direction.''
- ''Use a club on the ground for your alignment.''
- ''Practice your setup routine with each shot.''
- ''Take 2 practice swings between each swing, feeling the desired swing length for the distance.''
- ''Targets are set at 10-yard intervals from 60 yards through 160 yards.''
- ''Begin with a 5-iron (7- or 9-iron if not enough 5-irons) and work through the clubs.''

Student Options

- ''Play Bogey (see Step 4, Drill 5) with a partner of compatible ability.''
- ''With a partner, chart ball flight and distance with each club.''

Student Success Goal

- 70 total swings using different clubs in the following order and noticing the different distances the ball travels

    10 swings with a 5-iron

    10 swings with a 7-iron

    10 swings with a 9-iron

    10 swings with a 3-iron

    10 swings with a 7-wood

    10 swings with a 5-wood

    10 swings with a 3-wood

To Reduce Difficulty

- Let student place ball on tee.
- Only make golfer use a 7- or 9-iron.

To Increase Difficulty

- Have golfer work with a partner using the full swing checklist; golfer must meet 70% of the items correctly on 14 of 20 swings.

7. One-Leg Toe Drill
[Corresponds to *Golf*, Step 3, Drill 7]

Group Management and Safety Tips

- Review safety procedures for hitting and retrieving golf balls.
- All students may practice at one time, allowing for equipment and space.
- Line up students to swing and hit in the same direction.
- Place left-handers at right end of the line.
- Be sure space is appropriate for potential shot distances.
- Have 3 yards minimum between each hitting space or student.
- Partner work is effective.

Equipment

- Golf clubs, minimum 1 per student (5-, 7-, 9-irons, with extra 5- or 7-woods)
- Golf balls, 25 per student
- Tees, minimum 6 per student
- Targets, minimum 10 in the field

Instructions to Class

- "Feel the swinging motion of your arms and hands, with your body as a support."
- "If you lose your balance on the backswing or forwardswing, your body is too active."

Student Options

- "After 5 swings with balls on the ground, go back to hitting balls on a tee."
- "Hit toward targets, using the drill and playing Bogey with a partner (see Step 4, Drill 5)."

Student Success Goal

- 30 total swings in balance

    10 swings without a ball

    10 swings with a ball on a tee

    10 swings with a ball on the ground

To Reduce Difficulty

- Let student increase the balance support by placing the rear foot shoulder width apart and then moving the rear foot back of the target line, rather than placing the rear foot directly behind target foot.
- Have golfer alternate the regular full swing motion between each 2 repetitions of the drill.

To Increase Difficulty

- Make student hit all balls without a tee.
- Expand the Success Goal to include accuracy within 10 yards to the right or left of the selected target.
- Have golfer alternate between a wood and an iron.

8. *Shadow Drill*
[New drill]

Golf ball

Group Management and Safety Tips

- Review safety rules for hitting and retrieving balls.
- All students can practice at one time, allowing for equipment and space.
- Use a line formation with students swinging and hitting into a field.
- Have 3 yards between each swing station or student.
- This drill requires sunshine, but not in the middle of the day (the shadow must be long enough).
- This drill can be modified for indoors with a strong light source (e.g., a spotlight or camera lights) and golf mats.

Equipment

- Golf clubs, 1 per student (5-, 7-, or 9-irons, 5- or 7-woods)
- Golf balls, 1 per student (plastic or hard)
- The sun or a very bright light source if indoors with golf mats

Instructions to Class

- "To help you feel and see your swing, turn or pivot around a center while using your shadow as a living video."
- "Turn and face your shadow directly. Take your setup position and use an iron to place a ball in the middle of your head's shadow, which should be in the middle of your stance."
- "Practice your full swing, keeping your head's shadow on the ball. Be sure to make your full turn and weight shift."

Student Options

- "Practice with a wood. Is there a difference in the wood and iron shadow swing?" [*Teacher's note*: For a wood, the ball should be just outside the head's shadow due to ball placement at target side of center. Shadow moves to ball on follow-through with weight shift.]
- "Practice the One-Leg Toe Drill with the shadow."

Student Success Goal

- 15 swings keeping the head's shadow on the golf ball

To Reduce Difficulty

- Not applicable

To Increase Difficulty

- Have student practice with a partner, making swings with eyes closed and the partner relating whether the head remained on the ball.
- Make golfer use One-Leg Toe Drill or Two-Bucket Drill (Drill 9) with eyes open.

9. *Two-Bucket Drill*
[New drill]

Group Management and Safety Tips

- Review safety rules for hitting and retrieving balls.
- All students can practice at one time, allowing for equipment and space.
- Use a line formation with students hitting into a field.
- Have 3 yards between each swing station or each student.
- Be sure buckets are stable.
- You may substitute blocks of wood or upside-down crates.
- Check for student with back problems; use low blocks for such a student.

Equipment

- Golf clubs, 1 per student (5-irons, or 5- or 7-woods)
- Buckets, 2 per student (or as available; substitute crates, steps, or any other object 6–12 inches tall)
- Targets in the field
- Golf balls, 10 per student
- Tees, minimum 6 per student

Instructions to Class

- ''The purpose of this drill is for you to feel your posture being maintained as you swing your arms.''

- ''Place two buckets slightly closer than your shoulder width. Stand on the bucket with your weight midstep to the balls of the feet. Bend over, maintaining flat back, and let the club touch the ground.''
- ''Practice making controlled swings of 1-to-1, 2-to-2, and 3-to-3 lengths, feeling your arm swing. Do not swing fast, because you could lose your balance. The club should brush the ground with each swing.''

Student Option

- ''Alternate regular full swings with 3-to-3 bucket swings, trying to feel your posture back and through.''

Student Success Goal

- 9 total swings

    3 swings, 1-to-1 swing length

    3 swings, 2-to-2 swing length

    3 swings, 3-to-3 swing length

To Reduce Difficulty

- Use shorter objects for student to stand on.

To Increase Difficulty

- Have student practice hitting teed balls.
- Make golfer swing with eyes alternately open and closed.
- Add targets in the field.

10. 2-Liter Drill
[New drill]

Group Management and Safety Tips

- Review safety rules for hitting and retrieving balls.
- All students can practice at one time, allowing for equipment and space.
- Use a line formation with students hitting into a field.
- Have 3 yards minimum between each swing station or student.
- Be sure students don't start water-fights!
- Keep towels handy.
- Use drill with full swing practice.

Equipment

- Golf clubs (5-, 7-, or 9-irons, or 5- or 7-woods)
- 10 two-liter plastic bottles with caps (fill about 3 inches or 1/4 with water or very fine, light sand or sawdust)
- Extra water, sand, and/or sawdust
- Towels
- Targets

Instructions to Class

- "The 2-Liter Drill enables you to feel the effect of centrifugal force during the golf swing."
- "The 2-liter bottle is 1/4 full with water [or light sand]."
- "When you swing, as long as your arms and hands continue the swinging motion and your body moves in response to your arms, the water will stay in the bottom of the bottle. If the swinging motion is interrupted, the water will rush out of the bottle and you will get wet!"
- "This is the same principle as swinging a full bucket of water in a circle and not losing a drop."
- "Practice first with the cap on with each hand alone; then test yourself by taking the cap off."

Student Options

- "Alternate the 2-Liter Drill with full swings with a club."
- "Practice swinging with two bottles, one bottle with its cap on in each hand."

Student Success Goal

- 20 total full swings

  5 swings, rear hand, cap *on* bottle

  5 swings, target hand, cap *on* bottle

  5 swings, rear hand, cap *off* bottle

  5 swings, target hand, cap *off* bottle

To Reduce Difficulty

- Let student leave cap on the bottle at all times.

To Increase Difficulty

- Have student swing with eyes alternately open and closed.
- Reduce swings required with cap on the bottle to 6, and increase swings with cap off the bottle to 14.
- Make golfer swing two bottles (one in each hand) with the caps off at the same time.

Step 4 Learning From Ball Flight

Golf instruction has changed dramatically over the past 10 years. Students have become active learners in golf classes through a higher level of understanding of the golf swing. By learning to recognize ball flight influences, they develop control of their swings. With your help, they can become self-learners.

As you observe your students, their ball flights tend to be erratic in the early stages until they begin to feel the swinging motion. Getting the body moving and the club swinging in sync sometimes takes awhile. Initially, consistency in any direction is desired. Consistency is an indication that a pattern of movement is developing. Long, straight shots are the dream of the future! Refinement is more easily attained when some pattern has developed.

The ball flight rating scale and the Keys to Success (see *Golf: Steps to Success*) provide some guidelines as you observe your students.

STUDENT KEYS TO SUCCESS

- Square clubface at contact
- Controllable but rapid speed
- Angle of approach matches club
- Square contact
- Square path (or slightly inside out)

Ball Flight Rating

CRITERION	BEGINNING LEVEL	INTERMEDIATE LEVEL	ADVANCED LEVEL
Distance Clubface Club Speed Angle of Approach Squareness of Contact	• More open • Uncontrolled • Steep or shallow • Inconsistent	• More open • Variable • Shallow • Inconsistent	• Square to closed • Controlled • Controlled • Center
Direction Path Face	• Outside • More open slice	• Outside • More open slice	• Inside • Square to slightly closed draw

Error Detection and Correction for Ball Flight

The desire to achieve distance is the second major source of errors (after alignment), committed by golfers of all skill levels. These errors tend to be exhibited in an overactive upper body and shoulders on the forwardswing, and active hands in all phases of the swing. As you observe your students, observe them from directly in front, facing them, and from down the target line on the rear side.

ERROR ⊘

CORRECTION

1. There is inconsistent shot distance and direction, due to an overswing caused by the target hand grip letting go at the top of the backswing.

1. Suggest gripping the club with a penny under the little finger of the target hand, and swinging and hitting balls without letting the penny drop.

ERROR

CORRECTION

2. Tendency to hook or pull the ball exists, due to a wrist position at the top of the backswing, which often results from the wrists hinging on the backswing, away from the target line, called a convex wrist position.

2a. Have student practice all parts of the Cocking Drill (Step 3, Drills 4 and 5) to feel the appropriate wrist motion.

  b. Tell golfer to maintain the grip pressure in the last three fingers of the target hand.

3. Student has a tendency to push or slice the ball, due to target wrist position at the top of the backswing, which is often caused by the rear-side wrist flexing toward the target line, called a concave wrist position.

3a. Recommend the Cocking Drill (Step 3, Drills 4 and 5).

  b. Have golfer practice swings with the rear arm only, feeling the desired position at the top.

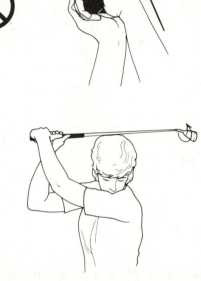

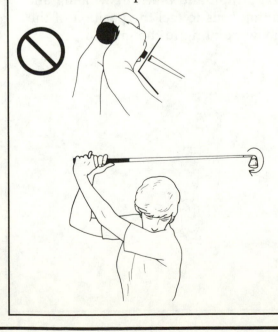

ERROR    **CORRECTION**

4. There is a high, weak pull, fade, or slice, due to rerouting the club from the inside swing path on the backswing to the outside swing path on the forwardswing (from an overactive upper body).

4. Set clubs on the ground as guidelines for the forwardswing. Student should angle the club in the direction of a push and feel as though pushing the ball.

5. Golfer has tendency to push shots with a low trajectory, due to the rear elbow pointing back rather than down, causing the rear hand grip to let go, then regrip, on the forwardswing (a flying elbow).

5a. Have student place a penny under the fat pad at the base of the thumb and practice swinging and hitting balls while keeping the penny in position.

b. Have golfer place a towel under the rear armpit and practice swinging and hitting balls to feel the position of the elbow pointing to the ground.

ERROR

CORRECTION

6. Inconsistent distance and direction off the tee, due to an incomplete backswing caused from lack of weight shift and body rotation.

6a. Recommend the Body Rotation Drill (Step 1, Drill 2).

b. Tell student to try to visualize shoulders turning 90 degrees as arms swing back, and feel hips turn as long as the arms are swinging.

Selected Learning From Ball Flight Drills

1. Long-Short Drill
[Corresponds to *Golf*, Step 4, Drill 1]

Group Management and Safety Tips

- Review safety procedures.
- Be sure the practice space is appropriate for the shot distances.
- Partner work is effective.

Equipment

- Golf clubs (5-, 7-, 9-irons, 5- or 7-woods)
- Extra clubs for alignment
- Golf balls, 25 per student
- Tees, 10 per student
- Targets
- Ball flight charts

Instructions to Class

- "On the golf course, you need to make swings that vary in speed in order to control the distance the ball travels."
- "By practicing various swings with the same club, you can begin to feel and see the effects of swing speed on the distance and trajectory of the ball."
- "Before each swing with a ball, make two practice swings, rehearsing the swing speed."
- "Use alignment clubs as you practice. Go through your setup with each swing."

Student Options

- "Practice with a partner charting the ball flight direction and distance with each club and speed."
- "Analyze the chart, noting ball flight tendencies with various speeds and clubs."

Student Success Goals

- 9 total shots, varying the speed of the swing to make the ball travel different distances

    3 speeds with a 9-iron

    3 speeds with a 5- or 7-iron

    3 speeds with a wood or long iron

- Long takes a fast swing speed
- Short takes a slow swing speed
- Medium takes a normal swing speed

To Reduce Difficulty

- Make student practice only the fast and normal speeds.
- Allow golfer to use only the 5- and 7-irons.

To Increase Difficulty

- Have student use only one club. Increase the total balls to 27 and add a distance consistency requirement to the Success Goal, for instance, 60% of the balls hit at each speed must cluster within 10 yards of each other.

2. Pop-Up Drill

[Corresponds to *Golf*, Step 4, Drill 2]

Group Management and Safety Tips

- Review safety procedures.
- Partner work is effective.
- A variety of obstacles is motivating and realistic.

Equipment

- Golf clubs (5- and 7-irons)
- Golf balls, 25 per student
- Targets (obstacles to hit over, such as volleyball or badminton nets)

Instructions to Class

- "On the course, you often hit balls under or behind obstacles and need to find ways to hit the shots."
- "Learn to alter the trajectory of your shots rather than resign yourself to having unplayable shots and taking penalty strokes."
- "Imagine a tea cup and a saucer; the sides of the tea cup represent a steep angle of approach, and the saucer the shallow angle. Your normal angle with an iron is between the two."
- "To create a steeper angle of approach, alter your swing arc on the backswing by swinging the club up sooner with your arms. To create a shallower angle, the swing arc is widened on the backswing by the club moving back along the ground longer on the backswing."
- "As you practice, visualize the tea cup and saucer."

Student Options

- "With a partner charting the ball flight, vary the angle of approach with each club."
- "Play Bogey, making a partner go over and under obstacles."

Student Success Goal

- 12 shots, making them travel at different heights by adjusting the angle of approach

    3 balls at a steep angle

    3 balls at a shallow angle

    3 balls at a normal angle

    1 ball at a steep angle

    1 ball at a shallow angle

    1 ball at a normal angle

To Reduce Difficulty

- Allow student to practice with only a 7-iron.
- Make golfer practice either the steep or shallow angle, but not both.

To Increase Difficulty

- Increase the total balls required to 24 and add distance control to the Success Goal—using one club, 50% of the balls hit with each angle of approach must cluster within 10 yards of each other.

3. Slice and Hook Drill
[Corresponds to *Golf*, Step 4, Drill 3]

Group Management and Safety Tips

- Review safety procedures.
- Check field space for enough width to practice hooks and slices.
- Practice balls stuffed with cloth or hose are excellent substitutes for hard balls in confined space.
- Partner work is effective.

Equipment

- Golf clubs (5-, 7-, and 9-irons)
- Golf balls, 25 per student
- Tees, minimum 6 per student
- Targets (set at 10-yard intervals from 60 to 160 yards)

Instructions to Class

- "The curvature of the shot is controlled by the position of the club at contact with the ball. Your hands and wrist action control the clubface."
- "Place an alignment club on the ground."
- "Grip the club and take your setup position with the club behind the ball in a square position. This creates a straight ball flight."
- "Open the clubface; note that this places the heel of the club ahead of the toe. This creates a slice. When the grip pressure is tight, your hands are less active and the slice occurs."
- "Now close the clubface; note that the toe of the club is in front of the heel. This position creates a hook. A light, but not loose, grip pressure helps to produce a hook."
- "Make 2 practice swings before each shot and try to visualize the desired clubface position and grip pressure when you imagine contacting the ball."

Student Options

- "Play Bogey with a partner."
- "Chart the ball flight curvature with each club. Is the amount of curvature the same with different clubs? Is there a difference in the distances between a hook and a slice?"

Student Success Goal

- 28 slices and hooks hit by adjusting the angle of the clubface for contact with the ball

  5 slices

  5 hooks

  5 straight shots

  3 slices

  3 hooks

  3 straight shots

  1 slice

  1 straight shot

  1 hook

  1 straight shot

To Reduce Difficulty

- Let student practice with only one club.
- Have golfer practice only hooks and straight shots.
- Let student use tees.

To Increase Difficulty

- Have golfer practice trying to curve the ball into a target.
- With a partner, student could select and record the desired shot prior to hitting, and record the results of the shot. What percentage of the desired shots were executed properly? Is there a bias?

4. *Two-by-Four Drill*
[Corresponds to *Golf*, Step 4, Drill 4]

Group Management and Safety Tips

- Review safety procedures.
- Allow students to choose between boards, boxes, and golf bags.

Equipment

- Golf clubs (3-, 5-, 7-, and 9-irons, 5- or 7-woods)
- Golf balls, 25 per student
- Tees
- Two-by-four boards, golf bags, cardboard boxes

Instructions to Class

- "The swing path at ball contact determines the starting direction of your ball. Developing consistency in the swing path helps you predict where to aim when you play golf."
- "At present your swing path may vary. With practice your consistency will develop in one direction—right, left, or straight. Eventually shooting toward the target is the most desirable."
- "This drill helps you begin to feel and see the desired swing path."
- "Select either a golf bag, cardboard box, or a two-by-four board; aim your box or board toward a target."
- "Begin with short swings to get used to the box or board. It will not hurt if you hit the board. Hit it a few times so you can feel the contact."
  [*Note*: Demonstrate ball position and swing path.]
- "Make 2 practice swings before each swing. Use your setup procedure with each swing."

Student Option

- "Practice with a partner checking alignment and charting ball flight path. Is there a difference between clubs? Is there a bias in direction?"

Student Success Goal

- 15 shots in a row, 3 with each club, in the following order without touching the board during the swing

  3 shots with a 5-iron

  3 shots with a 7-iron

  3 shots with a 9-iron

  3 shots with a 3-iron

  3 shots with a wood

To Reduce Difficulty

- Only make student use a 7-iron.
- Golfer may use tees.
- Let student start 3 or 4 inches from the board, gradually moving closer.

To Increase Difficulty

- Tell student to use a cardboard box and make practice swings with eyes closed.
- With student using one club, add consistency to the Success Goal: 65% of the shots must start in the same direction, for instance.

5. *Bogey Challenge*
[Corresponds to *Golf*, Step 4, Drill 5]

Group Management and Safety Tips

- Review safety procedures.
- Allow students to choose between playing Bogey individually or with a partner.
- Pair up students by ability (prepare pairs before class).

Equipment

- Golf clubs (5-, 7-, 9-irons, 5- or 7-wood)
- Golf balls, 25 per student
- Tees
- Targets

Instructions to Class

- "To play Bogey, one person in a pair selects a particular shot to hit, working on either curvature, path, or combinations of curvature and path (such as a pull-hook)."
- "If the selected shot is executed, the partner must try to hit the same shot. If successful, the process repeats. If unsuccessful, the partner is penalized with the next letter in the word *Bogey*; then the process repeats."
- "If the person selecting the shot is unsuccessful, then the partner selects, etc."

Student Options

- "Whoever wants to can play a round-robin."
- "Alternate clubs with each shot."

Student Success Goal

- Have partner acquire the 5 letters in *Bogey* first; one letter is earned for each shot missed.

To Reduce Difficulty

- Let golfer practice individually, recording the selected shot prior to hitting and then recording outcome.
- Golfer tallies the percentage of shots hit as selected and notes bias in execution.
- Allow use of tees for all shots.
- Let student use a 5- and 7-iron only.

To Increase Difficulty

- State that the same shot may not be selected twice in a row.

Step 5 Pitching

The pitch shot should be introduced to your students as a partial full swing, part of the whole swing concept discussed in Steps 1 and 2. You should reinforce the positive transfer of techniques from the full swing to the pitch shot. This will enhance their skill development in both the full swing and pitch.

As a result of the positive transfer of technique, many beginning students will display the characteristics of intermediate players quickly. However, for some students, this facilitation takes longer. The following criteria and the Keys to Success in *Golf: Steps to Success* provide you with guidelines in observing and working with students of various skill levels.

STUDENT KEYS TO SUCCESS

- Continuous motion
- Pendulum swing
- Fluid and smooth

Pitching Rating			
CRITERION	**BEGINNING LEVEL**	**INTERMEDIATE LEVEL**	**ADVANCED LEVEL**
Preparation **Setup** **Alignment** **Grip Pressure** **Ball Position** **Stance**	• Inconsistent • Closed or erratic • Tight • Varies • Too wide	• More consistent • More consistent (closed bias) • Less tight • More consistent	• Very consistent • Square alignment (to slightly open) • Light • Consistent
Execution **Backswing** **Forwardswing**	• Inconsistent length • Target arm bends • Fast pace • Active upper body • Decelerates at ball	• Consistent arc • Less restricted • More controlled • Accelerates to ball	• Consistent arc • Fluid motion • Accelerates to ball

Error Detection and Correction for Pitching

The errors you observed in your students in the full swing will also be evident in the pitch shot. The pitch being a partial full swing, your students will not suddenly develop new habits as they move to it from the full swing; the stroke habits are all interwoven. As you observe your students and note the consistency of their techniques in the full swing and pitch, point out the desirable or undesirable techniques to them. This helps facilitate transfer of good technique.

ERROR 🚫

CORRECTION

1. Pulled shots exist, due to an outside-in swing path; there is no body rotation or weight shift.

1. Recommend the Body Rotation Drill (Step 1, Drill 2).

🚫

ERROR   **CORRECTION**

2. There are fat or thin shots due to an early release on forwardswing.

2. Recommend the Cocking Drills (Step 3, Drills 4 and 5).

3. Low trajectory and fade shots exist, due to no wrist cock on backswing.

3. Check for tight grip pressure and recommend the Tee-Down Drills (1 and 2) to emphasize the release. First let the student place the ball on a tee for quick success, then move the ball to the ground.

ERROR   **CORRECTION**

4. There are fat or thin shots due to lateral movement of upper body on forward-swing.

4a. Recommend that your student use the One-Leg Toe Drill (Step 3, Drill 7) with a 3-to-3 and 4-to-4 swing length to feel the upper-body rotation.

b. Place a shaft in the ground, positioned over the ball on the outside of the target line. Have student make swings and feel turn around a center.

5. There are fat or thin shots due to excessive bend in target arm on back-swing, no turn or weight shift.

5. Have golfer practice 1-to-1, 2-to-2, and 3-to-3 swing lengths focusing on the target arm extension and weight shift as the swing length increases.

   **CORRECTION**

6. Push shot results from an inside-out swing path.

6. Recommend the Tee-Down Drills (1 and 2).

7. There are fat or thin shots due to excessive bend in target arm on backswing, no turn or weight shift.

7. Recommend practicing 1-to-1, 2-to-2, and 3-to-3 swings to feel the swing arc widen or increase arm extension with weight shift.

Selected Pitching Drills

1. Tee-Down Drill
Without a Ball
[Corresponds to *Golf*, Step 5, Drill 1]

Group Management and Safety Tips

- Review safety procedures.
- All students can practice at once if there are enough clubs.
- Use a line formation with 3 yards between students.
- Have all students swing in same direction.

Equipment

- Golf clubs (SWs, PWs, and 9-irons)
- Extra clubs for alignment
- Tees, at least 4 per student

Instructions to Class

- "Place a tee in the end of the grip of a pitching wedge, sand wedge, or 9-iron."
- "Rehearse the release motion of the hands and arms used in the 3-to-3 swing length. [*Teacher's note*: See Step 3, Drills 4 and 5.] Note that the tee should be pointing to the ground on the backswing (length 3) and at the end of the forwardswing (length 3)."
- "Place a club on the ground for alignment."

Student Options

- "Alternate between 3-to-3 and 4-to-4 swing lengths."
- "Select between 10 and 20 repetitions to practice at your own pace."

Student Success Goal

- 10 swings with good form and balance

To Reduce Difficulty

- Not applicable

To Increase Difficulty

- Have student swing with eyes alternately open and closed.
- Increase the desired swing length to 4-to-4.
- Make golfer alternate between 50% and normal swing pace.

2. Tee-Down Drill
With a Ball
[Corresponds to *Golf*, Step 5, Drill 2]

Group Management and Safety Tips

- Review safety procedures.
- Use line formation.
- Use partner system if space is limited.

Equipment

- Golf clubs (PWs, SWs, and 9-irons)
- Extra clubs for alignment
- Tees, at least 2 per student
- Golf balls, 20 per student
- Targets in field, 8–12 at 20, 40, and 60 yards

Instructions to Class

- "Place an alignment club on the ground."
- "Use your setup procedure before each shot. Make 2 practice swings before each shot."
- "Hold your follow-through until the ball stops rolling."
- "Watch for the desired ball flight: straight with a slight "draw.""

Student Options

- "After 10 swings (parts a–c) alternate between Tee-Down Drill and Pitch Shot."
- "Play Bogey with a partner (golf's version of Horse), aiming at different target distances on each shot."
- "Alternate between 3-to-3 and 4-to-4 swing lengths."

Student Success Goal

- 100 total swings with correct form, balls landing within 15 feet of target
  a. 40 swings with one club
     20 at 40-yard target
     20 at 20-yard target
  b. Repeat (a) with a different club
     20 at 40-yard target
     20 at 20-yard target
  c. Alternate clubs and targets
     20 shots, changing clubs and targets each time

To Reduce Difficulty

- Increase desired landing radius to 20 feet.
- Let student use a tee.
- Have golfer practice with only one club.

To Increase Difficulty

- Decrease desired landing radius to 10 feet.
- Increase shot distance to 50 and 60 yards.
- Add accuracy element to Success Goal—50% of shots must land within 15 feet of target, for example.

3. Alternate Swing Length Drill

[Corresponds to *Golf*, Step 5, Drill 3]

Group Management and Safety Tips

- Review safety procedures.
- Use a line formation.

Equipment

- Golf clubs (SWs, PWs, and 9-irons)
- Golf balls, 30 per student
- Tees
- Targets, 14 spaced at 10-yard intervals (20–90 yards)

Instructions to Class

- "The targets are set at 10-yard intervals from 20 to 90 yards."
- "Not everyone can hit a pitching wedge (PW) or sand wedge (SW) 90 yards with accuracy. Find *your* maximum distance with each club; reduce that distance to 85% and concentrate on accuracy and distance control."
- "Change targets and swing lengths every 3 or 4 swings."
- "Make 2 practice swings between each shot, feeling the swing length and swing pace for the next shot."

Student Option

- "After 20 shots, select a partner and play Bogey, selecting for distance and accuracy."

Student Success Goal

- 60 total swings
  - a. 3-to-3 swing length
    - 10 shots with a PW
    - 10 shots with a SW
    - 10 shots with a 9-iron
  - b. 4-to-4 swing length
    - 10 shots with a PW
    - 10 shots with a SW
    - 10 shots with a 9-iron

To Reduce Difficulty

- Allow student to put all balls on tees.
- Increase the desired landing radius to 20 or 25 feet.
- Only make golfer practice with one club.
- Reduce total swings required to 30.

To Increase Difficulty

- Make golfer vary swing pace (i.e., slower or faster than normal pace).
- Decrease desired radius of landing area to 10 feet.
- Have student practice with eyes closed, using a tee.

4. Variable Loft Drill
[Corresponds to *Golf*, Step 5, Drill 4]

Group Management and Safety Tips

- Review safety procedures.
- Use a line formation.
- As many students as clubs and space allow can practice at one time.
- This can be good indoor activity with plastic balls.

Equipment

- Golf clubs (PWs, SWs, or 9-irons)
- Golf balls, 15 per student (plastic or regular balls)
- Tees, 10 per student, with extras

Instructions to Class

- "Different situations during play on the course require controlling the loft of the ball, either higher or lower than the normal loft of the club."
- "Changes in ball position influence the natural loft of the club. A position forward of center adds loft, whereas a position back of center decreases loft."
- "Experiment with the loft of the PW, SW, and 9-iron by altering the ball position from center of stance, to off the target heel, or off the rear heel."

Student Options

- "Alternate between 4-to-4 and 3-to-3 swing lengths. What are the differences in loft and distance control?"
- "Record ball flight characteristics and distances with each club and ball position."

Student Success Goal

- 15 total swings

  5 swings, ball position off the target heel

  5 swings, ball position off the rear heel

  5 swings, ball position in the center of stance

To Reduce Difficulty

- Let student use tees.
- Only make student practice center and forward ball positions.

To Increase Difficulty

- Place obstacles at 20, 40, and 50 yards for students to hit over.
- Create safe landing areas bounded by imaginary hazards.

5. *Obstacle Visualization Drill*
[New drill]

Group Management and Safety Tips

- Review safety rules.
- Use a line formation.

Equipment

- Golf clubs (SWs, PWs, and 9-irons)
- Golf balls, 20 per student
- Tees, 10 per student, plus extras

Instructions to Class

- "On the golf course, the pitch shot is used whenever you need a relatively high trajectory and a shorter distance (20–90 yards) as you approach the green."
- "Practice visualizing a bush or bunker you need to hit over onto the green before each shot. See the location of the imagined obstacle in the practice area and focus on the desired landing area."
- "Limit your shot distance to a maximum of 50 yards."
- "Make 2 practice swings between each shot, feeling the swing pace for the desired distance."

Student Option

- "Play Bogey with a partner, picking a landing area and the desired trajectory."

Student Success Goal

- 15 total swings, visualizing the desired shot and distance before each swing

To Reduce Difficulty

- Let student use tees.
- Set up actual obstacles and targets.

To Increase Difficulty

- Have student visualize higher obstacles, such as trees.
- Have student visualize multiple obstacles, such as a bush to go over with water to the right of the green.
- Increase the distance to the landing areas, but not exceeding 85% of the student's maximum distance with the PW or SW, as established in the Long-Short Drill (Step 4, Drill 1).

Step 6 Chipping

Students can develop the chip shot technique fairly quickly because of the compactness and relatively restricted movement of the stroke. First emphasize the directional control on line short or long of the target. Stress the importance of using the setup procedure (Step 2, Drill 5) to develop a consistent technique.

You will observe a variety of skill levels in your class. The criteria listed below and the Keys to Success Checklist in *Golf: Steps to Success* may be used to guide your student evaluations.

STUDENT KEYS TO SUCCESS

- Pendulum swing
- Smooth, continuous motion

Chipping Rating

CRITERION	BEGINNING LEVEL	INTERMEDIATE LEVEL	ADVANCED LEVEL

Preparation
Setup
  Alignment
 	
  Ball Position
  Stance
  Swing Center
	• Inconsistent
	• Closed or erratic
	
	• Varies
	• Too wide
	• Behind ball
		• More consistent
		• More consistent (closed bias)
		• More consistent
			• Very consistent
			• Very consistent
			
			• Consistent

Execution **Backswing** **Forwardswing** **Release**	• Inconsistent length, usually too short • Stiff • Overactive upper body • Cocking wrist	• Consistent arc • Quiet upper body • More consistent one-unit swing	• Fluid motion • Unitary swing of hands and arms • Quiet upper body • One-unit swing (no release)
Follow-Through	• Stops at ball	• Length consistent with backswing	• Length consistent with backswing

Error Detection and Correction for Chipping

Chipping errors are easily detected and corrected because of the shortness of the stroke. There are fewer moving parts for the students to synchronize and for you to observe. The ball flight influences presented in Step 4 of the participant's book are primarily in direction and distance. Face and trajectory errors are minimized quickly with proper setup technique. The errors described below and those in the participant's book are the most commonly observed.

ERROR   **CORRECTION**

1. Ball travels beyond target, due to wrist cock on backswing. Swing length (3-to-3) too long for the shot distance needed.

1. Have student practice hitting balls with 2-to-2 and 1-to-1 swing lengths, noting the distances the ball rolls.

ERROR

CORRECTION

2. Fat or thin shot resulting from using wrist cock only on the backswing (*flippy wrists*).

2a. Golfer should hit shots only with arms to feel the lack of wrist cock, then use both hands together.

b. Recommend the Extended Club Drill (Drill 4).

3. Heeled, low shot goes to the right of target (to the left for a left-hander), due to closed alignment of shoulders, hips, feet, and clubface with a square path.

3. Tell student to practice taking square alignment using an alignment club on the ground and a club across the shoulders to feel and see the square position.

ERROR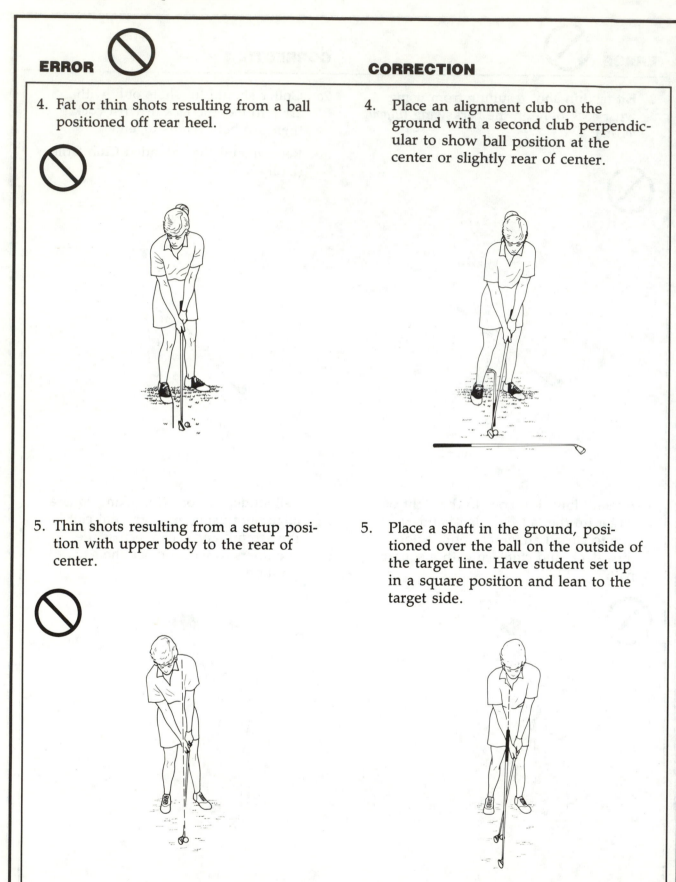

CORRECTION

4. Fat or thin shots resulting from a ball positioned off rear heel.

4. Place an alignment club on the ground with a second club perpendicular to show ball position at the center or slightly rear of center.

5. Thin shots resulting from a setup position with upper body to the rear of center.

5. Place a shaft in the ground, positioned over the ball on the outside of the target line. Have student set up in a square position and lean to the target side.

ERROR	**CORRECTION**
6. Push, or *shanked*, shots (ball contacts hosel) result from swing path inside on the backswing, due to hands alone initiating the backswing, rather than the unit of shoulders, arms, hands, and club together.	6. Recommend the Parallel Club Drills (2 and 3) for feeling the square path on the backswing and forwardswing. Golfer could alternate between drills and hitting shots.
7. There are pulled shots due to an outside-in swing path, resulting from using only arms without shoulders on swing.	7. Use Correction 6.

Selected Chipping Drills

1. Elephant Drill
[Corresponds to *Golf*, Step 6, Drill 1]

Group Management and Safety Tips

- Line up students facing the same direction.
- Scan one third of group at a time for correctness.
- All students can practice at the same time.

Equipment

- None

Instructions to Class

- ''Feel shoulders, arms, hand, and club work as a unit.''
- ''Minimize body motion without feeling as though you are 'in concrete.' ''

Student Option

- ''Work with a partner, using the Keys to Success Checklist.''

Student Success Goal

- 10 repetitions with fluid motion

To Reduce Difficulty

- Have student look into mirror during a swing.

To Increase Difficulty

- Vary the desired swing length from 1-to-1 to 2-to-2.
- Have student work with a partner and swing with eyes closed, maintaining the follow-through; your partner can tell you whether you had a balanced swing and the desired swing length.

2. *Parallel Club Drill Without a Ball*

[Corresponds to *Golf*, Step 6, Drill 2]

Group Management and Safety Tips

- Indoors: Line up students on two sides, swinging in opposite directions.

  Keep 3 yards between students.

  Keep students 6 yards away from sides or walls to facilitate your going around, scanning the group for corrections.
- Outdoors: All students face the same direction.
- All students can practice at once.
- Partner work is effective.

Equipment

- Golf clubs, a 7- or 9-iron for each student, plus 2 extra clubs or shafts per student
- Brush mats or carpet strips if indoors

Instructions to Class

- "Align parallel clubs toward a target."
- "Swing the club without contacting either of the parallel clubs."
- "Hold your follow-through each time to check for a square blade position and appropriate swing length."

Student Options

- "Alternate 1-to-1 and 2-to-2 swing lengths both with and without the parallel clubs."
- "After 5–10 repetitions of 1-to-1 and 2-to-2 swing lengths, work with a partner, using the checklist."

Student Success Goal

- 20 total repetitions with correct form

  10 swings, 1-to-1 swing length

  10 swings, 2-to-2 swing length

To Reduce Difficulty

- Remove one or both of the parallel clubs.
- Have student practice either the 1-to-1 or 2-to-2 swing length only.

To Increase Difficulty

- Have student swing with eyes closed.
- Have student work with partner and swing 1-to-1 or 2-to-2 swing lengths with eyes closed. With swinger holding the follow-through, partner relates whether swing lengths for backswing and forward-swing were appropriate and blade was square.

3. Parallel Club Drill With a Ball
[Corresponds to *Golf*, Step 6, Drill 3]

Group Management and Safety Tips

- Review safety procedures.
- Use a line formation.
- All students can practice at once, allowing for space and equipment.
- Partner work is effective.

Equipment

- Golf clubs (7- or 9-irons, with 2 extra clubs per student)
- Golf balls, 20 per student
- Targets set in a row 15 feet away from students

Instructions to Class

- "Swing the club without contacting either of the parallel clubs."
- "Check follow-through for square blade."
- "Note the differences in distance and height of ball flights."

Student Options

- "Alternate 1-to-1 and 2-to-2 swing lengths both with and without the parallel clubs."
- "Work with a partner after 5 to 10 repetitions, alternating 7- and 9-irons."

Student Success Goal

- 10 total pendular swings

  2 swings, 1-to-1 swing length

  2 swings, 2-to-2 swing length

  2 swings, 1-to-1 swing length

  2 swings, 2-to-2 swing length

  1 swing, 1-to-1 swing length

  1 swing, 2-to-2 swing length

To Reduce Difficulty

- Let student practice without ball.
- Have golfer practice either 1-to-1 or 2-to-2 swing lengths only.
- Remove target.

To Increase Difficulty

- Add targets at 10 and 20 feet.
- Remove tracks.
- Specify landing accuracy of within 5 feet of the target.

4. Extended Club Drill

[Corresponds to *Golf*, Step 6, Drill 4]

Group Management and Safety Tips

- Review safety procedures.
- Partner work is effective to check for extension. Use checklist.

Equipment

- Clubs, 2 per student (5-, 7-, or 9-irons)
- Golf balls, 20 per student
- Targets

Instructions to Class

- "It is important to know whether your arms, hands, and club maintain an extended position during the swing."
- "Take a regular grip on one club. Then grip a second club near its head as if it were an upward extension of the first club."
- "Swing this 'extra-long' club as if it were a regular club. Hold your follow-through to check arm and club position."
- "If the extended club hits your side on the forwardswing, you are using your wrist. Make practice swings until the club does not hit your side."

Student Options

- "After 5 or 10 repetitions, alternate with and without extended club."
- "Work with a partner, using the checklist."

Student Success Goal

- 20 total swings

    10 swings, 1-to-1 swing length

    10 swings, 2-to-2 swing length

To Reduce Difficulty

- Have student practice either 1-to-1 or 2-to-2 swing length only.
- Reduce swings required to 10.

To Increase Difficulty

- Make golfer hit balls with extended clubs.
- Add targets at 10, 15, and 20 feet.
- Specify landing accuracy of within 5 feet of the targets.

5. Ladder Drill
[Corresponds to *Golf*, Step 6, Drill 5]

Group Management and Safety Tips

- Review safety procedures.
- All students can practice at once, allowing for space and equipment.
- Partner work is effective.

Equipment

- Golf clubs, 5-, 7-, or 9-iron for each student
- Targets, 3 each at 10, 20, 30, and 40 feet (12 total)

Instructions to Class

- "Use an alignment club."
- "Vary the swing length and/or the swing pace to control the distance, and land the ball between the rungs on the ladder."
- "Make 2 practice swings between each ball."

Student Options

- "After 5 repetitions, work with a partner, using the checklist."
- "Play Bogey with a partner."

Student Success Goal

- 20 total shots

  7-iron

    2 shots, 1-to-1 swing length, landing between targets 1 and 2

    2 shots, 2-to-2 swing length, landing between targets 3 and 4

    2 shots, 1-to-1 swing length, landing between targets 2 and 3

  5-iron

    2 shots, 1-to-1 swing length, landing between targets 1 and 2

    2 shots, 2-to-2 swing length, landing between targets 3 and 4

    2 shots, 1-to-1 swing length, landing between targets 2 and 3

  7-iron

    2 shots, 1-to-1 swing length, landing between targets 2 and 3

    2 shots, 2-to-2 swing length, landing between targets 3 and 4

  9-iron

    2 shots, 1-to-1 swing length, landing between targets 2 and 3

    2 shots, 2-to-2 swing length, landing between targets 3 and 4

To Reduce Difficulty

- Have golfer practice with either a 7- or 9-iron only.
- Let student practice at 10 and 30 feet only.
- Reduce target lengths.

To Increase Difficulty

- Reduce target area to within 5 feet of target.
- Have student practice with a partner; require 75% correctness of items on checklist.

6. *Obstacle Drill*
[Corresponds to *Golf*, Step 6, Drill 6]

Group Management and Safety Tips

- Review safety procedures.
- Use a line formation.
- All students can practice at once, allowing for space and equipment.
- Set up stations for each club with the same obstacle height and targets, rotating students.
- This drill is effective indoors or outdoors.

Equipment

- Golf clubs, 7, 9, PW, or SW per student
- Golf balls, 20 per student
- Targets, 7

Instructions to Class

- ''Practice with 7, 9, PW, and SW to determine the most effective loft to clear the obstacle safely and roll close to the target.''
- ''Make 2 practice swings between each shot to feel the desired swing length and swing pace for the distance you want.''

Student Options

- ''Determine whether all clubs are effective for clearing the obstacle and rolling close to the pin at each distance.''
- ''After 5 or 10 repetitions, work with a partner, using checklist.''
- ''After 5 or 10 repetitions, play Bogey with a partner.''

Student Success Goal

- 20 total chips, with 10 balls landing within 10 feet of the desired targets

    3 chips, 15 yards from target

    3 chips, 20 yards from target

    3 chips, 25 yards from target

    2 chips, 15 yards from target

    2 chips, 20 yards from target

    2 chips, 25 yards from target

    1 chip, 15 yards from target

    1 chip, 20 yards from target

    1 chip, 25 yards from target

    1 chip, 20 yards from target

    1 chip, 15 yards from target

To Reduce Difficulty

- Have student use the 9-iron only.
- Use one target at 15 yards.
- Increase landing radius to 15 feet.

To Increase Difficulty

- Place several obstacles at varying heights.
- Reduce target radius to 5 feet.

Step 7   Putting

The basic techniques used in putting are readily developed. You can become very effective in analyzing the putting stroke, using the rating scale below and the Keys to Success in *Golf: Steps to Success* to guide your observations.

STUDENT KEYS TO SUCCESS

- Pendular swing
- Smooth, fluid motion

Putting Rating

CRITERION	BEGINNING LEVEL	INTERMEDIATE LEVEL	ADVANCED LEVEL

Preparation
Setup
  Alignment
 	
  Grip
  Posture
	• Inconsistent
	• Closed or erratic
	
	• Too light
	• Too tall
	• Eyes inside target line
		• More consistent
		• More consistent (open bias)
		• Inconsistent
			• Very consistent
			• Square
			
			• Moderate tension
			
			• Eyes over target line

Execution **Backswing** **Forwardswing**	• Inconsistent length • Overuse of wrists • Inconsistent pace • Active upper body	• Consistent length • Arms, wrists, hands, club as unit • Inconsistent pace • Less active upper body	• Controlled length • Unit • Consistent pace • Quiet upper body
Follow-Through	• Too short	• Length consistent with backswing	• Controlled

Error Detection and Correction for Putting

The errors you will observe in putting are generally similar to errors in the previous strokes; they usually occur from misalignment and/or overactive hands and shoulders. As you begin to observe your students, focus your correction on the setup and alignment. Use alignment clubs and the Parallel Club Drills (Step 6, Drills 2 and 3) to aid in developing the unitary stroke. Once the setup is developed, focus on the swing path, then work on distance control.

ERROR 🚫

CORRECTION

1. Pull from a square alignment exists due to outside-in swing.

1. Recommend the Track Drill (Drill 3) for feeling the path. Student should alternate every 3 strokes with the parallel clubs to 3 strokes without.

ERROR   **CORRECTION**

2. Push from a square alignment due to inside-out swing path.

2. Recommend Track Drill (see comments in Correction 1).

3. Pull from a square alignment due to wrist action opening blade on backswing and closing blade on forwardswing.

3. Have student practice the Cross-Hand Drill (Drill 8) to feel one unit (arms, hands, and club) back and through.

ERROR 🚫   **CORRECTION**

4. Ball curves to right on a straight putt, due to outside-in swing path from a setup position of open shoulders and a square blade.

4a. Have golfer practice the setup procedure using an alignment club on the ground and one across the shoulders.

  b. Student could practice the path with parallel clubs.

5. There is a pull due to shoulders initiating the forwardswing.

5. Recommend the Arm Swing Drill (Drill 1) for feeling the arms and hands swing with the shoulders still or inactive.

ERROR ⊘

CORRECTION

6. Inconsistent distance and direction result from shoulders tilting on the backswing and forwardswing, shutting the blade on the backswing and opening the blade on the forwardswing.

⊘

6. Recommend the Arm Swing Drill (see previous correction).

7. There is inconsistent distance and direction due to the wrist shutting and opening the blade during the stroke without the arm motion.

⊘

7. Recommend the Arm Swing Drill (see Correction 5).
[*Note*: The problem result is the same as in Error 6, but the cause is different.]

Selected Putting Drills

1. Arm Swing Drill
[Corresponds to *Golf*, Step 7, Drill 1]

Group Management and Safety Tips

- All students can practice at one time.
- Use a circle formation to facilitate your corrections, students' rear shoulders to inside of circle, 3 feet between students.

Equipment

- Golf clubs, 1 putter per student

Instructions to Class

- "Rehearse the motion of the putting stroke, feeling the arms and hands working as a unit during each phase."
- "Relax the shoulders. The shoulders are inactive, or still, through the swing."

Student Option

- "After 5 repetitions, work with a partner."

Student Success Goal

- 20 total swings
    - 10 swings without a club
    - 10 swings with a club

To Reduce Difficulty

- Not applicable

To Increase Difficulty

- Have student practice with eyes closed.

2. Eye Drill
[Corresponds to *Golf*, Step 7, Drill 2]

Group Management and Safety Tips

- All students can practice at one time, allowing for equipment.
- Indoors, use mats to protect floor.

Equipment

- Golf balls, 2 per student
- Golf clubs, 1 putter for each student (or pair of partners)
- Tennis balls, 1 per student

Instructions to Class

- "After you drop the ball from the bridge of your nose, hold your posture."
- "If the ball does not hit the ball or the line, readjust your posture and redrop the ball to check on your new setup."

Student Option

- "After 5 repetitions, work with a partner."

Student Success Goal

- 10 repetitions with correct form, the dropped ball landing on the ball or the putting line 7 of 10 times

To Reduce Difficulty

- Student may drop a tennis ball.
- Have golfer work with a partner.

To Increase Difficulty

- Make golfer close eyes after setup.

3. Track Drill, Option A
[Corresponds to *Golf*, Step 7, Drill 3]

Group Management and Safety Tips

- All students can practice at one time, allowing for equipment.
- Line up students in opposite directions to facilitate corrections.
- Partner work is effective.

Equipment

- Golf clubs, 1 putter per pair of students
- Extra clubs, 2 per pair of students
- Golf balls, 2 per student
- Carpet strips if indoors

Instructions to Class

- "Rehearse the three phases of the putting motion."
- "Hold the follow-through to check for a square blade and the position of the arms and hands."

Student Option

- "After 10 repetitions, work with a partner, using the checklist."

Student Success Goal

- 20 putting strokes without hitting either of the parallel clubs

To Reduce Difficulty

- Modify the Success Goal to require not hitting the clubs only 14 of 20 times.

To Increase Difficulty

- Make student practice with eyes closed.
- Have golfer practice with the rear and target arm separately, then as a unit.

Track Drill,
Options B and C

Group Management and Safety Tips

- Line up students in opposite directions to facilitate observations and corrections.
- Partner work is effective.

Equipment

- Golf clubs, 1 putter and 2 extra clubs per pair of students
- Putting cups
- Putting green or carpet strips if indoors
- Golf balls, 2–10 per pair of students

Instructions to Class

- "The objective is to make 10 putts in a row from each distance, then move to a longer distance."
- "Each time a putt is missed, begin a new set of 10. For example, if you have made 5 in a row from 2 feet and miss the 6th, start over again."
- "Make 2 practice strokes between each putt, feeling the smooth swing of the coming putt."

Student Options

- "After 7 putts made at each distance, work with a partner, using the checklist."
- "With a partner, chart the distance and direction of all putts."

Student Success Goals

- Option B: 30 total consecutive putts
    10 putts from 1 foot
    10 putts from 2 feet
    10 putts from 3 feet
- Option C: Remove the tracks and practice putting balls starting at 1 foot and moving back to 6 feet.

To Reduce Difficulty

- Modify Success Goal to require only 7 of 10 from each distance.

To Increase Difficulty

- Make student practice with eyes closed after the setup.
- Extend distances to 6 feet in units of 1 foot every 10 successful putts (Success Goal should be 60% for 3- to 6-foot putts).
- Let golfer make only one practice stroke between putts.

4. *Tape Drill*

[Corresponds to *Golf*, Step 7, Drill 4]

Group Management and Safety Tips

- All students can practice at one time, allowing for adequate equipment.
- Line up students in opposite directions to facilitate corrections.
- Partner work is effective.

Equipment

- Golf clubs, 1 putter for each pair of students
- Golf balls, 2 per student
- Tape
- Marking pens

Instructions to Class

- "The Tape Drill will help you develop a feel for the putting stroke by visually identifying the desired swing lengths on the markings on the tape (i.e., 1, 2, 3), and then matching the feel to the swing lengths."
- "Before you begin, take your setup position and use the Eye Drill (Drill 2) to check your posture and alignment."
- "Rehearse each swing length feeling the arms, hands, and club working as a unit."
- "On the first 2 repetitions at each length on the tape (i.e., 1-to-1, 2-to-2, 3-to-3), hold the backswing and follow-through to *feel* and *see* the desired swing lengths."

Student Options

- "Work with a partner, using the checklist."
- "Chart ball distances, noting consistency in stroke."

Student Success Goal

- 30 total strokes
  a. 15 strokes without ball
    5 strokes at 1-to-1 length
    5 strokes at 2-to-2 length
    5 strokes at 3-to-3 length
  b. 15 strokes with ball, using a practice stroke before each
    5 strokes at 1-to-1 length
    5 strokes at 2-to-2 length
    5 strokes at 3-to-3 length

To Reduce Difficulty

- Only make student practice the 1-to-1 and 3-to-3 swing lengths.

To Increase Difficulty

- Increase swings required for each swing length from 5 swings to 10.
- Have golfer swing, alternately opening and closing eyes.
- Working with a partner, student should take setup, close eyes, and relate to partner the swing length about to be made. Student then asks partner to determine the accuracy of the swing length.
- Have student alternate repetitions with and without tape.

5. Putting Ladder Drill

[Corresponds to *Golf*, Step 7, Drill 5]

Group Management and Safety Tips

- All students can practice at one time, allowing for equipment.
- Line up students in opposite directions to facilitate corrections.
- Partner work is effective.

Equipment

- Golf clubs, 1 putter per pair of students
- Golf balls, 6 per student
- Targets (tape, tee, clubs, putting cups, etc.)
- Carpet strips, if indoors

Instructions to Class

- "Make a practice stroke between each stroke. Feel the distance you want the ball to roll."
- "Then take a smooth putting stroke to the ball."

Student Options

- "Work with a partner, using checklist."
- "Set Success Goal of 75% of the items on the checklist met on 10 of 15 strokes."
- "Play Bogey selecting putts."

Student Success Goal

- 15 total putts for distance, attempting to make the balls stop rolling between the desired club distances

    3 putts at 10 feet

    3 putts at 13 feet

    3 putts at 16 feet

    3 putts at 19 feet

    3 putts at 22 feet

To Reduce Difficulty

- Modify Success Goal to 10 total putts, 2 at each distance.
- Increase distance between targets to 4 feet.

To Increase Difficulty

- Decrease target area to 1 foot.
- Make student putt for a desired distance with eyes closed.
- Add accuracy to Success Goal, requiring putt to roll between the desired club distances 9 out of 15 putts, for instance.

6. Cluster Putting
[Corresponds to *Golf*, Step 7, Drill 6]

Group Management and Safety Tips

- All students can practice at one time, allowing for equipment.
- Use scatter formation for independent work.
- Partner work is effective.

Equipment

- Golf clubs, 1 putter per pair of students
- Golf balls, 3 or 6 per student
- Carpet strips, if indoors

Instructions to Class

- ''To become a good putter, you need to develop a repeating stroke in both technique and the amount of swing pace and length, in order to control the distance and direction of putts.''
- ''Focus on the feel of the stroke, the swing length, and the swing pace.''

Student Option

- ''With a partner, putt the first ball without looking at the result. Putt the next 2. Based on the feel of the putt, estimate whether the ball went longer, even with, or shorter than the first. Partner replies to estimation. The objective is to feel the differences in the strokes and match the feel to the result.''

Student Success Goal

- 15 total putts in groups of 3, focusing on developing a feel for the repeated stroke

    3 putts to location A (1st ball)

    3 putts to location B (4th ball)

    3 putts to location C (7th ball)

    3 putts to location D (10th ball)

    3 putts to location E (13th ball)

To Reduce Difficulty

- Let student look at the distance each ball rolls.
- Modify Success Goal to 16 total putts in groups of 4; have student alternately look at the distance each ball rolls, then keep the eyes closed. Repeat for four different distances.

To Increase Difficulty

- Make golfer putt with eyes closed.
- Intensify Success Goal by requiring 9 of 15 to cluster within 1 foot.

7. Line Drill
[Corresponds to *Golf*, Step 7, Drill 7]

Group Management and Safety Tips
- All students can work at once.
- Use scatter formation for independent work.

Equipment
- Golf clubs, 1 putter per pair of students
- Golf balls, 6 per student
- Putting green or carpet strips
- Putting cups, if using carpet strips

Instructions to Class
- ''This drill will help you begin to feel consistency in your stroke within 3 feet of the hole and to develop confidence.''
- ''Be sure to use your setup procedure for each stroke.''
- ''Use the ball drop to check eye alignment before starting.''

Student Options
- ''Play Bogey with a partner, getting a letter for each restart.''
- ''Chart your putts: record those made; record short, long, right, or left of target for those you don't make.''

Student Success Goal
- 5 repetitions of 6 putts made in a row

To Reduce Difficulty
- Reduce Success Goal to require making only 5 of 6 balls.
- Reduce repetitions required to 3.

To Increase Difficulty
- Alternate each line of 6 balls, putting with only the rear hand, then the target hand, and finally both.
- Make student putt, alternately opening and closing eyes (take setup, then close eyes).
- If on a green, have golfer practice on various slopes.

8. Cross-Hand Drill
[New drill]

Group Management and Safety Tips

- All students can work simultaneously, alone or with partners.
- Use scatter formation.

Equipment

- Golf clubs, 1 putter per pair of students
- Golf balls, 6 per pair of students

Instructions to Class

- "The purpose of the Cross-Hand Drill is to help you reduce wrist motion in your putting stroke."
- "The rear hand tends to overpower the target hand."
- "Hold the putter with the target hand at the bottom end of the grip, and hold it against the target forearm with the rear hand. Make practice strokes, feeling the shaft and target arm as *one*."
- "The club shaft should maintain full contact with the target forearm throughout the stroke. If the club shaft comes off the forearm at any point during the stroke, you are using your wrists too much."
- "Position the ball about 3 inches from the target heel."

Student Options

- "Alternate between 1-to-1 and 2-to-2 swing lengths."
- "Practice the Cluster Drill with the cross-hand drill position."

Student Success Goal

- 16 total putts, with 2 practice swings between each putt

    5 cross-hand grip

    3 regular grip

    5 cross-hand grip

    3 regular grip

To Reduce Difficulty

- Require hitting only 3 cross-hand putts, and then 3 regular putts, etc.

To Increase Difficulty

- Make student putt, alternately opening and closing eyes.
- Have golfer alternate regular grip and the cross-hand grip, and do cluster putting.
- Have student putt for holes or at targets.

9. Green Clock Drill

[Corresponds to *Golf*, Step 7, Drill 8]

Group Management and Safety Tips

- Use a scatter formation.
- Partner work is effective.

Equipment

- Putting green
- Golf clubs, 1 putter per student or pair
- Golf balls, 6 per student

Instruction to Class

- "As you practice, note the differences in *where* the ball curves relative to the speed of the putt."

Student Options

- "After charting, analyze your putting. Do you have a bias in *direction* or *distance*? Do you make more putts on right-to-left or left-to-right breaks?"
- "Play Bogey with a partner."

Student Success Goal

- 12 total putts, charting the curvature of each putt as indicated by a dotted line on the clock face

To Reduce Difficulty

- Reduce total putts required to 8, 2 from each of the following positions: 12, 3, 6, and 9 o'clock.

To Increase Difficulty

- Increase the putting distance required to 8 feet.
- Have student alternate putts on clock between 5 feet and 8 feet (i.e., 12 o'clock = 8 feet, 1 o'clock = 5 feet, 2 o'clock = 8 feet).

Step 8 Sand Shots

As you observe and evaluate your beginning students' sand shots, your major focus should be on the students' ability to (a) *identify the type of lie*, either buried or resting on the sand, and (b) *take the proper setup position* consistently for the shot needed as determined by the lie. Once they have gotten into the setup position, the full swing motion is used.

Students should first focus on the objective of "getting out" of the sand at least 50% of the time. When this objective has been met 7 of 10 times during course play, their objective then is to practice "getting close," with-in 15 feet of the pin. The criteria in the rating and the Keys to Success in *Golf: Steps to Success* provide you additional guidelines for your observation and evaluation. The ball flight tendencies your students demonstrate in the full swing will be obvious in the sand shots.

STUDENT KEYS TO SUCCESS

- Smooth, continuous motion
- Displace the sand
- Swing through the sand and ball

Sand Shot Rating

CRITERION	BEGINNING LEVEL	INTERMEDIATE LEVEL	ADVANCED LEVEL
Preparation **Setup**	• Inconsistent	• More consistent	• Very consistent
Grip	• Inconsistent	• Consistent	• Very consistent
	• Excess tension in hands and arms	• Excess tension in hands and arms	
Alignment	• Closed or erratic	• More consistent (closed bias)	• Consistent
Ball Position	• Varies	• More consistent	• Consistent
Stance	• Too wide		
	• Digs in heels	• Digs in heels	• Digs in toes
Swing Center	• Behind ball		
Execution **Backswing**	• Inconsistent length	• More consistent	• Consistent
	• Stiff arm swing		
	• Restricted pivot		• Controls pivot
Forwardswing	• Overactive upper body	• Overactive upper body	• Controlled body
	• Restricted pivot	• Restricted pivot	• Limited pivot
	• Decelerates at ball	• Decelerates at ball	• Accelerates through ball
	• Lacks release	• Consistent	
Follow-Through	• Stops at ball	• More consistent	• Consistent

Error Detection and Correction for Sand Shots

Any swing problems students are experiencing in the full swing will be evident in the sand. As consistency comes in the full swing, sand shot control will also likely improve.

ERROR   **CORRECTION**

1. Ball stops short of desired distance, due to a steep angle of approach from an overactive upper body on forward-swing.

1. Have student widen the swing arc on the backswing to create a shallower angle of approach, maintaining the swing center through the ball.

2. Shots are *sculled* (hit thin) out of a trap, due to the swing center moving back on the forwardswing.

2. Recommend the One-Leg Toe Drill (Step 3, Drill 7) practiced in the sand for feeling the upper body remaining centered during the swing.

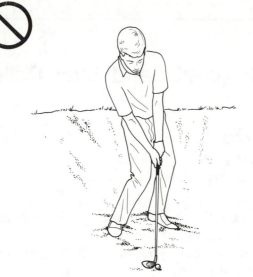

3. Fat shot due to a steep angle of approach, created by the arms with no wrist action.

3a. Recommend that the student practice the Cocking Drills (Step 3, Drills 4 and 5) in the sand to feel the arm and wrist action during the swing.

b. Golfer should focus on the bottom of the club "bouncing" off the sand, creating the opposite of a steep approach. Recommend practicing the Board Drill (Drill 7).

ERROR ⊘	CORRECTION
4. Fat shot due to incomplete backswing and upper body initiating the forward-swing (see Step 3).	4. Have student practice making a complete backswing, holding at the top to feel the position, then swinging "through" the sand.

Selected Sand Shot Drills

1. Sandy Line Drill: Explosion Shot
[Corresponds to *Golf*, Step 8, Drill 1]

Group Management and Safety Tips

- Review safety procedures. Be sure rakes are laid on ground with picks down.
- Be sure all students are hitting in the same direction.
- If the wind is blowing, contact lens wearers may want to wear goggles or switch to glasses.
- If no traps are available, a sand or sawdust jumping pit used for track is good for demonstration.

Equipment

- Golf clubs, 1 sand wedge (SW) or pitching wedge (PW) per student
- Rakes for the sand
- Balls, 10 per student
- Targets

Instructions to Class

- "As you take your setup for each swing, remember to
  - (a) open the blade slightly, then grip the club; and
  - (b) dig your toes slightly into the sand."
- "Use your regular full swing motion."
- "Be sure the ball is sitting on top of the sand."
- "Try to hit the sand out of the trap by hitting the sand, not the ball. Swing through the sand."
- "Rake the trap frequently; follow safety procedures for the rake."
- "Remember—your first objective is to get out of the sand."

Student Option

- "After 5 repetitions, work with a partner, using the checklist."

Student Success Goal

- 15 total swings with correct form

  10 swings hitting the sand at a consistent location relative to the line, without a ball

  5 swings at hit line, continuing through balls placed 1 inch to target side of line

To Reduce Difficulty

- Have student practice hitting the sand without worrying about the line.
- Have golfer focus on knocking sand out of the trap.

To Increase Difficulty

- Increase Success Goal to 8 of 10 shots with balls.
- Make student swing with eyes closed.
- Add targets.
- Have golfer try to vary the height of the shot by changing the angle of approach.

2. Sandy Line Drill: Buried Lie Shot

[Corresponds to *Golf*, Step 8, Drill 2]

Group Management and Safety Tips

- Review safety procedures.
- All students may practice at one time if hitting in same direction.
- Be aware of blowing sand in windy conditions.

Equipment

- Golf clubs, 1 SW, PW, or 9-iron per student
- Golf balls, 20 per student
- Rakes

Instructions to Class

- "Your first objective is to get out of the sand."
- "Practice your setup routine with each shot. Remember the differences between the buried lie shot and the explosion shot:
    - (a) ball position center to the rear,
    - (b) weight leans to target side, and
    - (c) club deflofted."
- "Use your regular full swing motion."
- "Dig your toes into the sand."
- "Rake the trap often."

Student Options

- "After 5 repetitions, play Bogey golf with a partner."
- "Experiment with the distance results by changing the ball position forward and backward in the stance."

Student Success Goal

- 15 total swings with correct form

    10 swings at a consistent location relative to a line (without a ball)

    5 swings on the line, balls buried on the "new" line

To Reduce Difficulty

- Student could practice hitting the sand without the ball between each swing with a ball.

To Increase Difficulty

- Make golfer hit for targets.
- Have student alternate between the explosion and buried lie shots.

3. Fried Egg Visual Image Drill for Explosion Sand Shot
[Corresponds to *Golf*, Step 8, Drill 3]

Group Management and Safety Tips

- Review safety procedures.
- Maintain 3 yards between students, all hitting in same direction.

Equipment

- Golf clubs, 1 SW or PW per student
- Rakes
- Golf balls, 20 per student

Instructions to Class

- "Remember to take the setup for an explosion shot."
- "Open the clubface first, then take your grip."
- "Feel the bounce of the club as you swing through the oval. Get the whole 'egg' out of the 'pan.'"

Student Option

- "Between each shot, close your eyes and visualize the club swinging through the oval."

Student Success Goal

- 5 ovals ("eggs") in the sand with a ball ("yolk") in the center of each, hitting each "egg" out of the sand

To Reduce Difficulty

- Have student practice hitting only the open oval.

To Increase Difficulty

- Modify the Success Goal to include hitting the ball out of the trap from the oval 7 of 10 times.
- Make the golfer use the Overlap Drill (Drill 4) between regular swings.

4. Overlapping Grip Sand Drill: Explosion Shot
[Corresponds to *Golf*, Step 8, Drill 4]

Group Management and Safety Tips

- *Caution*: If any student has a problem with subluxation (dislocation) of the target shoulder, he or she *should not* let the rear hand off after impact as indicated to increase difficulty.
- Review safety procedures.

Equipment

- Golf clubs, 1 SW, PW, or 9-iron per student
- Rakes
- Golf balls, 20 per student
- Targets

Instructions to Class

- "The overlapping grip will initially feel weak and strange. Remember—your rear hand completely covers your target hand."
- "The purpose of this drill is to help you identify the motion of your target arm during the swing."
- "The tendency in the sand is to hit fat shots, due to the target arm slowing down or stopping on contact with the sand. Feel the target arm swing through the sand."
- "Rake the trap often."

Student Options

- "Take full swings, alternating the regular grip and the overlapping grip."
- Play Bogey with a partner, calling for different distances."

Student Success Goal

- 15 total swings with the correct form

    10 swings hitting the sand in the same spot 7 of 10 times

    5 swings hitting the sand line and continuing through balls placed 1 inch to the target side of the line

To Reduce Difficulty

- Modify the Success Goal to 10 total swings

    6 swings hitting the sand, 3 of 6 times in same spot

    4 swings hitting sand line and continuing through the ball placed 1 inch to the target side of the line

To Increase Difficulty

- Increase the balls hit in the Success Goal to 10.
- Have student let the rear hand off after impact.
- Add an accuracy element to the Success Goals, such as requiring landing within 18 feet of the target.

5. Overlapping Grip Sand Drill: Buried Lie Shot

[Corresponds to *Golf*, Step 8, Drill 5]

Group Management and Safety Tips

- *Caution*: If anyone has a problem with a dislocating shoulder (subluxation), this student should not let the rear hand off at impact as suggested to increase the drill's difficulty.

Equipment

- Golf clubs, 1 SW, PW, or 9-iron per student
- Golf balls, 20 per student
- Rakes
- Targets

Instructions to Class

- "In the buried lie, you will feel the resistance of the sand more than in the explosion shot."
- "Maintain your arms and hands swinging *through* the sand."

Student Options

- "After 5 swings at the sand only, begin hitting balls in each type of lie."
- "Play Bogey with a partner, calling for different distances."

Student Success Goal

- 15 total swings with proper setup

   10 swings hitting the sand at consistent location relative to the line

   5 swings at balls slightly buried on the target line

To Reduce Difficulty

- Allow student to alternate the regular full swing with the Overlapping Drill swing.
- Let golfer practice either the buried lie or explosion shot.

To Increase Difficulty

- Increase the total swings to 20.
- Have the student let the rear hand off after impact.
- The golfer could vary the pace of the swing from normal to 50%, noting differences in distance.

6. *Bunker Distance Drill*
[Corresponds to *Golf*, Step 8, Drill 6]

Group Management and Safety Tip

- Review safety procedures.

Equipment

- Golf clubs, 1 SW, PW, or 9-iron per student
- Golf balls, 25 per student
- Rakes

Instructions to Class

- "Practice your setup routine with each shot."
- "Notice the difference in the length of the swing or speed needed to produce bunker shots traveling from 5–30 yards."

Student Options

- "Practice with a partner, charting directions and distances of shots."
- "Practice with a partner, using the checklist."
- "Play Bogey with a partner, selecting any one or a combination of (a) distance, (b) direction, and (c) type of shot.

Student Success Goal

- 24 total shots, 3 shots at each distance for each type of shot

  Explosion Shot

  3 balls hit at a 5-yard target

  3 balls hit at a 10-yard target

  3 balls hit at a 20-yard target

  3 balls hit at a 30-yard target

  Buried Lie Sand Shot

  3 balls hit at a 5-yard target

  3 balls hit at a 10-yard target

  3 balls hit at a 20-yard target

  3 balls hit at a 30-yard target

To Reduce Difficulty

- Have golfer hit for the 10-yard target only.
- Student may hit for either distance or accuracy initially, not both.

To Increase Difficulty

- Make golfer alternate between a buried lie and explosion shot.
- Expand the Success Goal to require accuracy to within 15 feet of the pin on 6 of 12 shots.

7. Board Drill
[New drill]

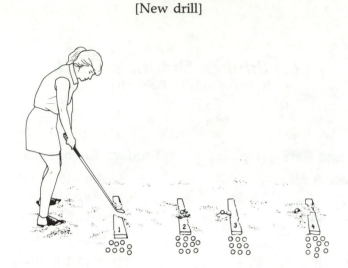

Group Management and Safety Tips

- Review safety procedures.
- Board should be completely buried, level with the sand's surface
- *Caution*:
  - (a) Pile the sand on the middle or target end of the board.
  - (b) Keep extra balls at the end of the board to mark it, so students will not hit the end.
  - (c) Use sand wedges or pitching wedges only, because they have a wide sole.

Equipment

- Golf clubs, 1 SW or PW per student
- Golf balls, 20 per student
- Rakes
- Boards, 1 per sand station (two-by-fours or two-by-sixes)

Instructions to Class

- "The Board Drill will help you learn how to use the 'bounce' or wide sole of the sand wedge for the explosion shot."
- "Look at the bottom of the sand wedge. Note how the bottom is wider and lower than the front edge."
- "Remember to open the blade slightly, then take your grip."
- "Use your regular full swing motion."
- "Listen for the sound the 'bounce' makes on the board."

Student Options

- "With a pile of sand and a ball on the board, practice varying your swing pace. Note the distances the balls travel."
- "Vary the number of balls hit off the board and off the regular sand."

Student Success Goal

- 20 total swings with correct form

  5 swings hitting the pile of sand off the board

  5 swings hitting the pile of sand and ball off the board

  5 swings hitting the pile of sand and ball off the sand

  5 swings hitting the ball off the sand

To Reduce Difficulty

- Let student use a very broad and flat board
- Only make golfer hit off the board.

To Increase Difficulty

- Add targets.
- Expand Success Goal to require accuracy to within 15 feet of the target 10 of 20 shots.

Step 9 Uneven Lies

Practice opportunities for the uneven lies can be difficult to find in most practice areas. This can create frustration both in teaching these skills and in giving feedback to students about their execution of the skills.

However, it is possible to determine their *understanding* of the principles of uneven lie shots. Whenever observation is possible, you can use the following criteria as well as the Keys to Success and the Keys to Success Checklist in *Golf: Steps to Success*.

STUDENT KEYS TO SUCCESS
- Fluid motion
- Shoulders and body posture follow the contour of the land

Uneven Lies Rating: Uphill and Downhill Lies

CRITERION	BEGINNING LEVEL	INTERMEDIATE LEVEL	ADVANCED LEVEL
Preparation **Setup** Alignment	• Inconsistent • Shoulders not parallel to slope	• More consistent	• Very consistent
Ball Position Weight	• Varies • On low foot	• More consistent • Inconsistent	• Consistent • On high foot
Execution **Backswing**	• Inconsistent length, usually too long • Fast pace • Inconsistent wrist cock	• Consistent arc • Consistent cocking	• Fluid motion
Forwardswing	• Body out of sync with arm swing • Body moves faster than balance can accommodate • Early uncocking	• Body timed with arm swing • Body less active • Inconsistent uncocking	• Body motion integrated with arm swing • Timed release integrated with arm swing and body motion
Follow-Through	• Excessive, with body turn	• More controlled	• Compatible with slope

Uneven Lies Rating: Sidehill Lies, Ball *Above* Feet

CRITERION	BEGINNING LEVEL	INTERMEDIATE LEVEL	ADVANCED LEVEL
Preparation **Setup** 　Grip 　Alignment	• Inconsistent • Gripped at end of club • At target	• More consistent • Grip choked-up • At target	• Consistent • Grip choked-up • At intermediate target
Execution **Backswing** **Forwardswing**	• Inconsistent • Length uneven • Body out of sync with arm swing • Restricted lower body	• Consistent • Length matches slope severity • Timed better	• Consistent • Length matches slope severity • Good timing
Follow-Through	• Excessive for slope on forwardswing		• Matches slope

Uneven Lies Rating: Sidehill Lies, Ball *Below* Feet

CRITERION	BEGINNING LEVEL	INTERMEDIATE LEVEL	ADVANCED LEVEL
Preparation **Setup** 　Posture	• Inconsistent • Too erect	• Inconsistent • Erect	• Consistent • Posture matches slope severity
Execution **Backswing** **Forwardswing**	• Inconsistent length • Swing too long • "Ball bound" • Lower body restricted • Upper body moves first and too fast	• Inconsistent • Swing shortens • Inconsistent • Pace varies	• Fluid • Appropriate length • Target awareness • Body integrated with arm swing
Follow-Through	• Out of balance	• Balanced	• Body accommodates for slope • Controlled

Error Detection and Correction for Uneven Lies

Uneven lies create frustrating situations for beginners. Most errors here are the result of lack of adjustment in the setup position for the slope of the lie. Full swing errors noted in your students also appear in the uneven lie shots. As with the sand, errors tend to be magnified, due to the special balance and setup conditions caused by the slope.

ERROR

CORRECTION

1. Student tops the ball on *downhill lie*, due to lack of body rotation and weight shift.

1a. Recommend that the student practice Body Rotation Drill (Step 1, Drill 2) on a downhill lie.

   b. Have student practice 3-to-3 swing length to feel rotation and weight shift.

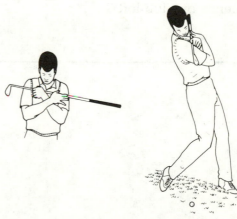

ERROR 🚫

CORRECTION

🚫

2. Golfer tops the ball on *uphill lies*, due to reverse weight shift.

2a. Suggest practicing Body Rotation Drill (Step 1, Drill 2) on an uphill lie.

b. Have golfer practice 4-to-4 swing length, holding follow-through to feel balance.

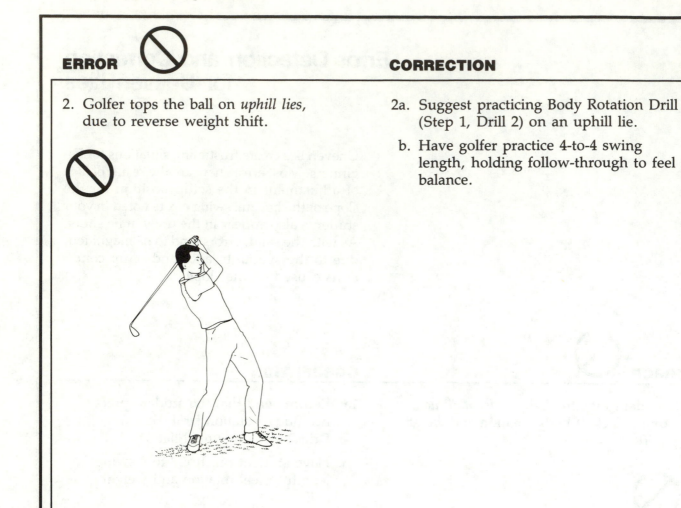

3. Student hits *downhill lies* consistently long, due to lack of considering slope influence on club loft.

3. Have student select club one number higher when hitting downhill because the slope tends to decrease the club loft.

ERROR 🚫   **CORRECTION**

4. Student tops *sidehill lies* with ball above the feet, due to lateral movement of the body on the backswing, rather than pivoting (see Error 1).

4a. Have student practice Body Rotation Drill (Step 1, Drill 2) on a sidehill lie.

b. Have golfer practice 4-to-4 swing length for control.

5. Golfer slices *sidehill lie* below the feet, due to not uncocking the wrist and stopping at the ball (because of loss of balance, weight moved toward toes).

5. Recommend practicing the One-Leg Toe Drill (Step 3, Drill 7) on a sidehill lie, starting with the ball on a tee, then without.

🚫

Selected Uneven Lie Drills

1. Setup Sidehill Lie Drill
[Corresponds to *Golf*, Step 9, Drill 1]

Group Management and Safety Tips

- Review safety procedures.
- Use a line formation.
- All students can practice at one time, allowing for equipment and space.
- Partner work is effective.
- Plastic balls are effective substitutes for golf balls when you're using the back side of practice tee areas.

Equipment

- Golf clubs, one 5-iron per student (supplement with 7- or 9-irons, if desired)
- Extra clubs or shafts, 2 per student (for alignment)
- Golf balls or plastic balls, 20 per student
- Targets

Instructions to Class

- "Review the checklist as you practice your setup position."
- "Make practice swings to determine your ball position and to establish a feel for balance."

Student Options

- "After 5 repetitions on each lie with a 5-iron, experiment with other lofted clubs noting the differences in loft of each club and its results on the distance of ball flight."
- "Hit shots with your normal setup from the various lies. What are the results for each shot?"

Student Success Goal

- 20 total swings, noting balance on the follow-through

   10 swings, sidehill lie with ball below feet

   10 swings, sidehill lie with ball above feet

To Reduce Difficulty

- Have student practice with the ball either above or below the feet only.
- Let golfer use a 7- or 9-iron only.

To Increase Difficulty

- Make golfer practice with a wood.
- Place several targets in the field and have student alternate targets.

2. Uphill/Downhill Lie Drill
[Corresponds to *Golf*, Step 9, Drill 2]

Group Management and Safety Tips

- Review safety procedures.
- Use a line formation.
- All students can practice at one time, allowing for equipment and space.
- Partner work is effective.
- Plastic balls are effective substitutes for golf balls when you're using the back side of the practice tee area.

Equipment

- Golf clubs, one 5-iron per student
- Extra clubs or shafts, 2 per student
- Golf balls or plastic balls, 20 per student
- Keys to Success Checklist from participant's book

Instructions to Class

- "Review the checklist as you practice the setup positions."
- "Make practice swings to determine your ball position and to feel your balance."
- "Set your shoulders to follow the contour of the slope."
- "Feel the club swing up or down the slope."

Student Options

- "After 5 repetitions with a 5-iron, experiment with other lofted clubs, noting the differences in loft and distance."
- "Alternate shots with your normal setup from the various lies. Chart the distances and ball flights. What are the effects?"

Student Success Goal

- 20 total swings, noting balance on follow-through

    10 swings with downhill lie

    10 swings with uphill lie

To Reduce Difficulty

- Require practicing either the uphill or downhill lie, only.
- Let student use a 7- or 9-iron only.

To Increase Difficulty

- Make golfer practice with a wood.
- Place several targets in the field and have student alternate targets.

3. Single Bucket Drill
[Corresponds to *Golf*, Step 9, Drill 3]

Group Management and Safety Tips

- Review safety procedures.
- Use a line formation.
- All students can practice at one time, allowing for equipment and space.
- Partner work is effective.
- Plastic balls are effective substitutes for real balls.

Equipment

- Buckets, 1 per pair of students
- Golf clubs, 1 per student (5-, 7-, or 9-iron, or 5- or 7-wood, traded around)
- Golf balls, 10 per student (hard or plastic)

Instructions to Class

- "Maintaining good balance is important in golf. The bucket drill is designed to emphasize any tendency to be off-balance."
- "Make 2 practice swings before each shot."
- "Focus on the differences in the shoulder alignment due to the elevated position."

Student Options

- "Make practice swings standing on one leg, with the other elevated as on a slope; alternate standing on left and right legs."
- "Work with a partner, using the checklist and attempting to get 75% of the items correct on 3 of 5 swings from each lie."

Student Success Goal

- 10 total swings

  5 swings with a 7-iron, rear foot on a bucket

  5 swings with a 5- or 7-wood, ball on a tee, and target-side foot on a bucket

To Reduce Difficulty

- Make student practice either uphill or downhill position only.
- Modify drill to 5 shots, with one regular full swing practice swing between each.

To Increase Difficulty

- Have golfer make practice swings with eyes closed.
- Place targets in the field to require shooting for direction.

4. Cluster Drill

[Corresponds to *Golf*, Step 9, Drill 4]

Group Management and Safety Tips

- Review safety procedures.
- Use a line formation.
- All students can practice at one time, allowing for equipment and space.
- Partner work is effective.
- Plastic balls are effective substitutes for real golf balls.

Equipment

- Golf clubs, 1 PW or 7- or 9-iron per student
- Golf balls, 10 per student (hard or plastic)
- Targets

Instructions to Class

- "Uneven lies occur frequently around the greens. Accuracy in these shots can help you lower your score quickly."
- "This drill will help you begin to feel the differences between your uneven lies setup positions and that of the full swing. Also, you'll learn to control the length of swing for various distances."
- "Balance is not affected as much on the shots around the green as on the full swing."
- "The setup is very important."

Student Options

- "After 3 shots from each lie, practice with a friend, using the checklist."
- "Play Bogey with a partner, coming closer to the target as each shot goal."
- "Chart your distance and direction with each shot. Then analyze your chart. Do you have any direction or distance tendencies? Does club selection affect the distance control on various lies?"

Student Success Goal

- 40 total swings, trying to group balls into 5-yard clusters
  - 20 pitch shots
    - 5 pitches from uphill lie
    - 5 pitches from downhill lie
    - 5 pitches from sidehill lie with ball below feet
    - 5 pitches from sidehill lie with ball above feet
  - 20 chip shots
    - 5 chips from uphill lie
    - 5 chips from downhill lie
    - 5 chips from sidehill lie with ball below feet
    - 5 chips from sidehill lie with ball above feet

To Reduce Difficulty

- Have student practice either chip or pitch shot, but not both.
- Expand target areas to 8-yard clusters.

To Increase Difficulty

- Expand Success Goal to 70% of the shots, and group into 5-yard clusters.
- Require that student demonstrate correct form on 75% of the items on the checklist on 6 out of 10 shots.

Step 10   Effective Practice

During your regular class sessions, you will often organize practice in a very structured fashion. This structure is probably essential if you are working in large groups, due to the importance of safety.

However, as teachers or coaches, it is our ultimate job to work ourselves *out* of a job by making learners self-sufficient. This step is designed to teach your golfers how to structure their own practices and to continue to learn between lessons. The rating scale indicates the overall areas of emphasis on which players of different skill levels should focus.

STUDENT KEYS TO SUCCESS

- Start each practice with warm-up
- Practice all shots each time
- Use variability of practice strategies
- Practice in gamelike conditions

Effective Practice Rating

CRITERION	BEGINNING LEVEL	INTERMEDIATE LEVEL	ADVANCED LEVEL
Warm-Up	• Total body flexibility • Arm strength	• Total body flexibility • Arm strength	• Total body flexibility • Hand and arm strength
General Practice Needs	• Emphasizes full swing rhythm and motion	• Emphasizes timing of swing	• Emphasizes various types of shots
Preparation Setup **Grip**	• Consistency • Relaxes tension in hands and arms	• Consistency • Relaxes in hands and arms	• Grip consistent • Balances tension between hands
Alignment	• Square	• Square (open for chip)	• Alignment varies for special shots
Ball Position	• Consistent ball position • Swing center over ball	• Consistent ball position • Swing center over ball	• Consistent ball position • Swing center over ball
Posture	• Stance shoulder width • Tends to sit back on heels	• Weight midstep to balls of feet	• Well-balanced

CRITERION	BEGINNING LEVEL	INTERMEDIATE LEVEL	ADVANCED LEVEL
Execution **Backswing**	• Consistent length • Too short • Stiff	• Consistent arc • On path	• Fluid motion • Unit swing
Release	• Lacks arm rotation on forwardswing • Quiet upper body (not overactive)	• Quiet upper body	• Quiet upper body
Forwardswing **Release**	• On path • Cocking wrist	• On path • More consistent cocking and un-cocking	• Consistent cocking and uncocking
Follow-Through	• Full swing through ball	• Backswing and forwardswing equal length	• Balanced swing lengths

Error Detection and Correction for Effective Practice

Practice sessions in golf should emphasize the skills you are trying to teach. It is easy for students to continue to practice the full swing motion with their ''favorite'' clubs. Unfortunately, golf does not allow players to use favorite clubs all the time. It is therefore important that each golfer practice all the clubs that will be used.

A good practice session should have specific goals (review Step 16). If you are using this as a general practice session, then all clubs should be practiced for their specific purposes. On the other hand, if you are really focusing on one club, then a systematic sequence to work on that skill is necessary.

The following errors reflect problems that are often seen in practice strategies. Be on the lookout for these tendencies in your golfers.

ERROR

| CORRECTION |

1. Golfer is always looking around at other golfers or looking to see if others are watching.

1. Emphasize that everyone is his or her own teacher during practice. Each golfer should practice both strengths and weaknesses.

ERROR 🚫	CORRECTION
2. Student seems to practice best shots most of the time.	2. Set aside a specific time during practice when everyone works on their weakest skills (e.g., not everyone has to be hitting 9-irons at once).
3. Student seems to get bored practicing and always wants to go out and play.	3. Use more challenges or games in practice, such as Bogey.
4. Student fails to use routine before each shot.	4a. Assign a partner to help check for use of routine.
	b. Suggest using a checksheet for each shot so golfer must record use of routine, club used, resultant ball flight, and mental aspects of shot.
5. Alignment problems persist during practice.	5a. Always have alignment clubs available.
	b. After each shot, student should lay down club across front of toes and go behind to check alignment.

Selected Effective Practice Drills

1. Routine Practice
[Corresponds to *Golf*, Step 10, Drill 1]

Group Management and Safety Tips

- Review safety procedures.
- Have all students face and hit in the same direction.
- Partner work is effective.

Equipment

- Golf balls, 20 per student
- Golf clubs, 2 per student (5- and 7-irons)
- Targets, 5–9 spread out

Instructions to Class

- "Using the same routine before every shot is an important key to golf."
- "Your routine signals your body that you are ready to hit and guarantees that you start from the same foundation each time."

Student Options

- "Select a different target each time."
- "Work with a partner, who times and checks routine sequence."

Student Success Goal

- 20 shots using correct routine each time

To Reduce Difficulty

- Allow alignment clubs.
- Provide markers for intermediate targets.

To Increase Difficulty

- Vary target each time.
- Allow partners to distract.
- Make student change clubs each time.
- Remove alignment clubs.

2. Varying the Target Drill
[Corresponds to *Golf*, Step 10, Drill 2]

Group Management and Safety Tips

- Review safety procedures.
- Have all students face and hit in the same direction.
- Have all swing *or* pick balls at the same time.

Equipment

- Golf clubs, 1 per student (5- or 7-iron)
- Extra clubs, 1 per student for alignment
- Balls, 20 per student
- Targets, 10 spread out in practice area

Instructions to Class

- "Learning to aim at different targets is critical in golf."
- "The key to good shots is to use the same preshot routine, focusing on alignment."
- "Practice hitting to different targets in the field. Start by hitting to the same target 5 times in a row, so you can check on alignment. Then vary the target with each shot."

Student Options

- "Select different targets."
- "Work with partners."

Student Success Goal

- 20 total swings toward targets
  - 5 swings straight ahead
  - 5 swings to a target to the left
  - 5 swings to a target to the right
  - 1 swing straight ahead
  - 1 swing to left
  - 1 swing to right
  - 1 swing to left
  - 1 swing straight ahead

To Reduce Difficulty

- Place alignment clubs on ground.
- Provide intermediate target markers.
- Have golfers work in pairs to help check alignment.

To Increase Difficulty

- Dictate which targets must be shot at.
- Allow partners to distract.
- Use uneven lies.

3. Varying the Club Drill
[Corresponds to *Golf*, Step 10, Drill 3]

Group Mangagement and Safety Tips

- Review safety procedures.
- All students should face and hit in same direction.
- Have all hit *or* pick up balls at the same time.
- Put targets at different distances. Have students start with 5-irons to determine which target is right for that club. Then tell them to hit to next closer target for the 7-iron and one longer for 3-iron (avoid yardage labels).

Equipment

- Golf clubs, 3 per student or partner trio (3-, 5-, and 7-iron)
- Golf balls, 25 per student (or partner group)
- Targets, placed at 5 different distances: 80, 100, 120, 140, and 160 yards (to allow for different distance abilities of students)

Instructions to Class

- "You seldom hit the same golf club 2 times in a row. It is important to learn to hit different clubs to targets at varying distances."
- "Begin by practicing one club 5 times in a row. Then hit the club only 2 times in a row, and finally once per club."
- "Because you are using different clubs, your targets will vary. Hit the 5-iron to the middle target, the 7-iron to the closest target, and the 3-iron to the target farthest away."

Student Options

- "Pick the clubs to be used."
- "Work with partners."
- "Determine how many shots to be hit at each target."

Student Success Goal

- 24 total shots with 3 different clubs and 3 different distance targets, using routine and hitting a good full swing on each shot

  5 swings with 5-iron to 120-yard target

  5 swings with 7-iron to 100-yard target

  5 swings with 3-iron to 150-yard target

  2 swings with 5-iron, 120 yards

  2 swings with 7-iron, 100 yards

  2 swings with 3-iron, 150 yards

  1 swing with 5-iron, 120 yards

  1 swing with 7-iron, 100 yards

  1 swing with 3-iron, 150 yards

To Reduce Difficulty

- Only make student use 2 clubs.
- Let golfer hit more balls in a row with the same club.

To Increase Difficulty

- Make student change clubs each swing.
- Require use of short irons and close targets for pitching and chipping.

4. Vary the Lie of the Ball Drill

[Corresponds to *Golf*, Step 10, Drill 4]

Group Management and Safety Tips

- Review safety procedures.
- Have students all face and hit in same direction.
- Have all hit *or* pick up balls at the same time.

Equipment

- Clubs, 1 per student (preferably a 3-, 5-, or 7-iron)
- Balls, 25 per student
- Practice area with some bare spots and divot holes
- Targets in hitting area

Instructions to Class

- "It is important to learn to hit a good golf shot when your ball is in a not-so-good, as well as a good, lie."
- "Practice hitting shots from bare ground, from grass, and from divot holes. Remember to use your routine, and take a good full swing at each."

Student Options

- "Use club of choice."
- "Choose your own order of hitting uneven lie shots."
- "Use uphill, downhill, and sidehill lies."

Student Success Goal

- 25 total swings from good and bad lies
    5 swings from good lies
    5 swings from bare spots
    5 swings from good lies
    5 swings from divots
    5 swings from good lies

To Reduce Difficulty

- Have student use shallow divot holes.
- Have student use soft bare spots.

To Increase Difficulty

- Make golfer alternate shots rather than repeat same lie.
- Add uphill, downhill, and sidehill lies to Success Goal.

5. *Opposites Drill*
[Corresponds to *Golf;* Step 10, Drill 5]

Group Management and Safety Tips

- Review safety procedures.
- Have entire group do the same shots in order (call them out).
- Partner work is effective.

Equipment

- Golf clubs, a 5- or 7-iron per student
- Golf balls, 36 per student
- Targets in the hitting area

Instructions to Class

- "When learning golf, it is important to know what causes each type of shot. In this drill, you will practice the extreme shots, such as slices and hooks, so that you can feel what it is like to hit one accidentally."
- "Practice hitting pairs of opposites. Hit the extremes to find the means to perfect shots."
- "Be sure to use your preshot routine and an intermediate target with each shot."

Student Options

- "Choose order of hitting shots."
- "Play Bogey (golf's version of Horse), calling for a slice, a push, and so on."
- "Use alignment clubs."

Student Success Goal

- 36 total shots, hitting each of a pair of non-straight shots 3 times, with at least 4 of 6 attempts correct in each pair

  6 shots, alternating slice and hook

  6 straight shots

  6 shots, alternating hitting on top and below ball

  6 straight shots

  6 shots, alternating push and pull

  6 straight shots

To Reduce Difficulty

- Have student hit only slices and hooks.

To Increase Difficulty

- Make student hit each shot with a different ball flight from the previous.
- Call out shot to be done on your command.

6. Pitch and Chip Drill
[Corresponds to *Golf*, Step 10, Drill 6]

Group Management and Safety Tips

- Review safety procedures.
- All students should face and hit in same direction.
- Set up obstacles to be hit over (e.g., volleyball nets).
- Partner work is effective.

Equipment

- Clubs, 2 per student (5- or 7-iron and PW or 9-iron)
- Targets at 10–15 yards
- Balls, 30 per student
- Obstacles (bags, boxes, buckets, etc.)

Instructions to Class

- ''For proficient golfers, the short game accounts for about 50% of the shots. It is important to practice the short game.''
- ''Practice the pitching and chipping shots by alternating clubs and swing lengths.''
- ''Remember the differences in the setup positions.''

Student Options

- ''The order of hitting pitches and chips is up to you.''
- ''Work with a partner.''
- ''Select your own target.''

Student Success Goal

- 30 total pitches and chips

  10 shots pitching with PW or 9-iron to 30- to 50-yard target

  10 shots chipping with 5- or 7-iron to 10-yard target

  3 shots pitching

  3 shots chipping

  2 shots pitching

  2 shots chipping

To Reduce Difficulty

- Let student hit all pitches first, then go to chips.

To Increase Difficulty

- Place obstacles in path for student to hit over.
- Make golfer alternate chip and pitch shots.

7. *Round of Golf Drill*

[Corresponds to *Golf*, Step 10, Drill 7]

Group Management and Safety Tips

- Review safety procedures.
- All students should face and hit in same direction.
- Specify area for putts.
- Work with partners or foursomes is effective.

Equipment

- Golf clubs, a full set per student (or per group sharing clubs)
- Golf balls, 20 per student
- Targets in the field to aid with alignment
- Scorecards from different courses (or diagrams of different holes)

Instructions to Class

- ''One way to effectively practice is to imagine that you are playing a round of golf, even though you are only in the practice area.''
- ''Start by imagining the first hole; perhaps it is a 400-yard hole with a series of bunkers on the left of the green but a good opening on the right. The fairway is wide open and does not have many hazards.''
- ''Decide what club to use for the first shot. Then actually hit a ball. Notice where it actually lands in the practice area, and imagine where that would have been in the imaginary fairway.''
- ''Once you have imagined your ball landing, decide what shot you should hit next—perhaps a 5-iron onto the green, and then actually hit a 5-iron. Continue hitting the shots that would be appropriate for the imaginary hole.''
- ''Finish each hole by taking out a putter, choosing a target on the practice area, putting the ball, and imagining it going into the hole.''

Student Options

- ''Select a scorecard from the different courses provided, and play the course in your mind.''
- ''Play with a partner; practice taking turns in the proper order, depending on where your shots land.''

Student Success Goal

- 9 holes of golf in your mind. Imagine a specific hole, select a different shot each time, and complete your actual routine before each shot.

To Reduce Difficulty

- Provide diagrams of holes to be played.

To Increase Difficulty

- Use uneven lies.
- Have partners call shots.

8. Chip and Putt Drill
[New drill]

Group Management and Safety Tip

- Review safety procedures.

Equipment

- Golf clubs, 1 putter per student and one 6- or 8-iron, PW, or SW per student (could substitute 5- or 7-irons)
- Golf balls, 1 per student

Instructions to Class

- "Using one ball, chip from various distances around the green to different pin placements. Use a 6- or 8-iron, PW, or SW for the chips."
- "After each chip, putt the ball into the hole. This is called getting 'up and down.'"
- "Keep track of the total strokes for each 'chip and putt' sequence."

Student Options

- "After 10 sequences, compete with a partner."
- "Experiment with a variety of club lofts to determine those most effective for different distances and lies."

Student Success Goal

- 20 sequences with 70% correct form and successfully chipping and 1-putting 50% of the time

To Reduce Difficulty

- Have student use either a 6- or 8-iron (not PW or SW).
- Reduce Success Goal percentage of successful chips and 1-putts to 40%.

To Increase Difficulty

- Increase percentage to 70%.
- Have student work with a partner, aiming for correct form on 70% of the checklist items on 6 out of 10 strokes.

9. Tic-Tac-Toe Game
[New drill]

Group Management and Safety Tips

- Review safety procedures.
- All students face and hit in the same direction.
- Put labels (numbers or letters) in the grid squares to make it easy to call shots.
- Grids can be made with lime (field marking techniques) or by placing cones at 20-yard intervals throughout the field.

Equipment

- Golf balls, 20 per pair of partners
- Handout with 12 tic-tac-toe diagrams, 1 per pair
- Tic-tac-toe target grids, 5 laid out on the field; each square in a grid should be 20 yards square
- Golf clubs, at least 2 per student (a variety of irons to correspond to distances on grid)

Instructions to Class

- "Learning to control the landing area of your ball is critical in golf."
- "With a partner, play a game of tic-tac-toe. You must call your shot ahead of time by telling your partner which square grid area is your target."
- "Using the sheet of paper with tic-tac-toe grids drawn on it, record your X or O if your shot landed in the right area."

Student Options

- "Predict the landing location of each shot."
- "Decide how many shots you allow in order to make the desired target (e.g., 1 or 3 tries)."

Student Success Goal

- 3 Xs or Os in a line, winning the tic-tac-toe game by landing your ball in the proper "squares"

To Reduce Difficulty

- Increase the size of the grid.
- Allow 3 shots in order to land 1 in the specified area.

To Increase Difficulty

- Make grid smaller.
- Use the final resting spot of the ball as the key rather than the landing location without the roll.
- Partner specifies the golfer's required landing location.

Step 11 Preshot Routines for Each Swing

Golf is a game of precision and control. Unlike many other sports, golf is a completely self-paced activity, with the start of each shot being timed exclusively by the performer. For this reason, golfers tend to take great care to have their minds under control before they start their swings.

A good golfer starts each swing in exactly the same way. Just like a basketball player who executes every free throw after the same number of preliminary bounces, a golfer goes through the same steps before taking every swing. For the golfer, this is even more important because the position relative to the target changes each time, whereas the basketball player always comes to the same line and the target is a stationary backboard. The following criteria will help you detect problems in the preshot routine in your golfers.

STUDENT KEYS TO SUCCESS
- Repeating same sequence every time
- Time remains consistent
- If interrupted, start entire sequence over again

Preshot Routine Rating

CRITERION	BEGINNING LEVEL	INTERMEDIATE LEVEL	ADVANCED LEVEL
Preparation **Setup** Grip	• Irregular grip • Position on club changes	• Grip consistent	• Consistent
Alignment	• Inconsistent set of feet, hips, shoulders	• Improving in consistency	• Consistent
Intermediate Target	• Poor use of intermediate target	• Uses more regularly	• Good target awareness
Attention Control	• Mentally distracted	• Focuses attention better	• Under mental control
Timing	• Total time varies • Shorter under stress	• Time more consistent	• Timing consistent

Error Detection and Correction for the Preshot Routines

Errors in the preshot routine are primarily those of omission. Many young golfers fail to use a routine at all, or else use a very erratic sequence of activities. The errors described below and in the participant's book are the most commonly observed.

ERROR 🚫

CORRECTION

1. The preshot routine is done in a different order each time.

1. Write down the order of the preshot routine on a 3 × 5 card; have the student read it out loud during each setup.

2. The golfer consistently picks the wrong club.

2. Have golfer review the order of "LTD" checks—*lie* of the ball, desired *trajectory*, and required *distance*—before selecting a club.

3. Alignment seems to be off to the right, and the ball always lands to the right of target.

3a. Have student check the club face and body alignment by using alignment clubs.

   b. Have golfer pick an intermediate target that is real. For instance, student can place a series of tees of different colors on the ground in front of the ball, draw an imaginary line from the ball to the target, and pick out the tee that falls on that line as the intermediate target.

4. Attention is distracted by other golfers talking.

4. Golfer must stop the routine at whatever point it is, go back to starting point, and repeat the entire routine sequence.

Selected Preshot Routine Drills

1. Intermediate Target Drill
[Corresponds to *Golf*, Step 11, Drill 1]

Group Management and Safety Tips

- Line up all students facing the same direction.
- If indoors, use lines on the gym floor to facilitate alignment.
- Use pieces of string attached to two tees instead of tape.

Equipment

- Tape, masking tape, ribbon, string
- Golf balls, 1 per student
- Golf clubs, 1 per student (5- or 7-iron)

Instructions to Class

- "Because golf is a target game, it is important to have a target for alignment purposes."
- "Stand behind the ball and find a target in the field. Imagine a line drawn between the ball and the target."
- "Locate a spot 8 to 12 inches along that target line. Place a piece of tape between the ball and the intermediate target."
- "Use entire routine. Line up the clubface and your body in relation to the intermediate target."
- "Repeat 10 times."

Student Options

- "Rehearse all aspects of the setup."
- "Hit balls at completion of setup."
- "Work with a partner; have partner stand behind you to check alignment."

Student Success Goal

- 10 repetitions with the intermediate target in line with the target

To Reduce Difficulty

- Paint lines on grass using water soluble spray paint. Be sure to check with maintenance prior to marking field. (Could use streamers in the grass as an alternative.)

To Increase Difficulty

- Have golfer change targets each time.
- Student could try to determine intermediate target by standing by side of ball rather than from behind ball.

2. *Partner Distraction Drill*
[Corresponds to *Golf*, Step 11, Drill 2]

Group Management and Safety Tips

- Review safety procedures.
- All students face and hit in the same direction.
- All objects used as distractions should be soft, and not subject to being airborne if golfer hits them accidentally (e.g., tissue paper, paper wads, golf gloves; do not use tennis balls, other golf balls, etc.).

Equipment

- Golf clubs, one 5-iron per student
- Extra tees, paper, noisemakers
- Golf balls, 10 per student

Instructions to Class

- "It is important to maintain your concentration during your entire routine. For you to practice this skill, your partner will attempt to distract you during your routine and shot."
- "Partners, try to distract each other. You may say anything that is not 'X-rated,' toss tees into the field of vision, sing, clap, make loud noises, and so on."
- "Hit 5 balls, then trade roles. Then keep switching until each of you has hit 10 balls."

Student Options

- "Golfer can choose the type of distractions used by partner."
- "Switch roles after each shot rather than after 5 shots."

Student Success Goal

- 10 balls hit while maintaining concentration in spite of partner's attempt to distract

To Reduce Difficulty

- Restrict partners to using only one distraction tactic at a time.

To Increase Difficulty

- Have students work in groups of 3 or 4, one person hitting and the others all distracting.
- Have golfer participate in the distractions. For instance, partners make word associations: One says "red," golfer replies with first thought; partner says "birdie," golfer says "eagle." As a team, partners can count backward by 3 from 100 while one player hits. Partners can sing songs in rounds (such as "Row, row, row your boat").

3. Circle Alignment Drill
[Corresponds to *Golf*, Step 11, Drill 3]

Group Management and Safety Tips

- All students face and hit in the same direction.
- Keep hitting stations at least 3 yards apart.
- Review safety procedures.

Equipment

- Golf balls, 10 per student
- Multiple targets in the field
- Golf clubs, 1 per student (5- or 7-irons)

Instructions to Class

- "In order to experience the shot variability caused by not using your routine, experiment with not using a routine."
- "Put a ball on the ground, walk up to it, and walk around it twice. Then immediately hit the ball without using your preshot routine. Hold the follow-through, then set your club down on the ground along your toes."
- "Walk behind the ball and determine whether you were aligned in the proper direction. Write down the direction of alignment (bias)."
- "Repeat this walkaround drill 10 times without using your routine. Record the direction of bias each time."
- "Then use your routine before each of 10 additional shots. Be sure to use an intermediate target each time."

Student Options

- "Choose multiple targets."
- "Choose the number of times to walk around ball."

Student Success Goal

- 20 total shots

    10 shots without using routine

    10 shots, using specific routine before each shot

To Reduce Difficulty

- Let student walk directly up to the ball (not around it 2 times).
- Have golfer use only one target for all 10 shots.

To Increase Difficulty

- Make student close one eye when taking setup.
- Have golfer take alignment, then change target and reestablish alignment.

4. Routine Timing Drill
[Corresponds to *Golf*, Step 11, Drill 4]

Group Management and Safety Tips

- Review safety procedures.
- Use a line formation.
- Remind timers to stay out of way of golfers.
- Provide instruction on the care and use of stopwatches.

Equipment

- Golf balls, 10 per student
- Stopwatches for half the class, or have students bring watches with a second hand (alternate strategy: Have one big clock that is visible to all students, such as the timing clock in the gym)
- Golf clubs, 5- or 7-irons for half the class

Instructions to Class

- "One key to a consistent routine is to do it in the same amount of time every time it is repeated."
- "Working with a partner, take turns timing each other's routine. The golfer must establish the point at which the timing should start (e.g., when picking up the club, when standing behind the ball, or when determining the intermediate target)."
- "Partner times the entire routine, stopping the watch when the ball is struck. Record the total time for each routine."

Student Options

- "Choose where to start routine timing."
- "Use either the same or variable targets."

Student Success Goal

- 10 repetitions of the same routine

    4 at regular speed

    3 at a faster than normal speed

    3 at regular speed, staying within 10% of average time established in the first 4 setups

To Reduce Difficulty

- Have student do all 10 repetitions at the normal speed.
- Keep the target the same for all shots.

To Increase Difficulty

- Allow the timer to try to distract the golfer (see Partner Distraction, Drill 2).
- Have golfer imagine various situations, for instance, the final hole of a tournament, playing in the rain, being rushed by golfers in the next foursome.
- Force golfer to interrupt routine and start over again.

Step 12 Preparing for a Round of Golf: Mental Skills

The mental skills of golf can be as important as the physical skills, for without the proper mental attitude, the physical skills cannot emerge. It is important to realize that physical skills are critical, for they determine the level of play. However, it is equally as important to develop the mental skills that will free the body to execute those skills. If a golfer is too tense, the hands and wrists cannot release, even though the skill has been learned. Similarly, if a golfer imagines negative thoughts, those thoughts influence the swing and the resultant ball flight.

STUDENT KEYS TO SUCCESS

- Tension controlled, moderate range of tension
- Positive thoughts
- Preshot routine to check tension and thoughts

Mental Skills Rating

CRITERION	BEGINNING LEVEL	INTERMEDIATE LEVEL	ADVANCED LEVEL
Tension Control **Detect Tension** **Control Tension**	• Unable to sense tension changes • Unable to control	• Beginning to sense tension • Some control by use of relaxation and breath control	• Sensitive to tension changes • Controls tension
Attentional Control **Control** **Use of Thought Stoppage**	• Cannot let go and then regain attention • Needs specific cue to focus on • Can identify negative thoughts • Uses trigger to interrupt • Hard to replace negative with positive thoughts	• Uses cue to regain attention (e.g., setting down bag) • Own cues for regaining attention established • Identifies negative thoughts • Uses trigger to interrupt • Some replacement of negative with positive thoughts	• Good attentional control • Attentional control good • Automatically stops negative thoughts • Uses trigger to interrupt • Replaces negative with positive thoughts

Error Detection and Correction for Mental Skills

The mental skills of golf should be practiced just like the physical skills. When a physical problem exists, it is often demonstrated by the ball flight or other things that can be observed by someone else. The real challenge exists with observing mental skills, which are hidden inside the golfer and must be interpreted by an "outsider."

In this section on mental errors, typical problems of golfers are described, with possible solutions suggested. However, it is important to realize that the real "diagnostician" of mental errors must be the golfer. You cannot see into the head like you can observe the swings!

ERROR

CORRECTION

1. After playing or practicing, golfer complains of a tight neck or shoulders.

1a. Suggest relaxation techniques to relieve tension in the shoulders and arms.

  b. Progressive relaxation works well: student should start by increasing tension to maximum while inhaling, then exhaling fully as the shoulder and arms release.

2. When your student has taken a setup position and you cannot move the club easily, it indicates too much tension (hint: At address, try to lift the club head toward the sky; if there is too much tension you will not be able to lift the club easily).

2a. Suggest relaxation techniques.

  b. Have golfer start with too much tension (level 5) and then slowly release (4) to the neutral tension level (3). (See Game of 5s, Drill 1.)

3. Golfer reports that when standing on the tee and seeing a water hazard, he or she envisions the ball landing in the water.

3. When a negative image occurs, student must be sure to stop it, then re-imagine a good shot landing in the desired target area.

4. Golfer seems to hit many slices.

4. Ask whether golfer feels tense. If so, where? Suggest relaxation techniques to regain optimal level.

ERROR

CORRECTION

5. Golfer has little rotation in the full swing; cannot see ''belt buckle'' on both the backswing and forwardswing.

5. Emphasize the importance of a relaxed swing. Also, you could actually help student rotate hips (manually, so full range is felt; see Step 1, Drill 2).

6. After a less than desirable (poor) shot, the golfer seems to be criticizing or berating himself, or herself.

6. Encourage golfer to recognize negative thoughts, use thought stoppage technique, and replace negative with positive thoughts or images.

Selected Mental Skills Drills

1. Game of 5s Drill
[Corresponds to *Golf*, Step 12, Drill 1]

Group Management and Safety Tips
- Review safety procedures.
- Use a line formation.
- Partner work is effective.

Equipment
- Golf balls, 25 per student
- 5- or 7-iron, one per student

Instructions to Class
- ''You can learn to control tension, just like you learn to swing a club at different speeds or for different swing lengths.''
- ''One of the problems in golf is that we do not have a good way to describe tension, so we must create our own scale. Imagine that a *5* is your maximum tension and a *1* is the minimum.''
- ''Make a fist with one hand as tight as you can; this is a *5*. Now, be as relaxed as possible in that same hand; this is a *1*.''
- ''It should be possible for you to create a *5* or *1*—or anything in between—in any body part.''

Student Options
- ''Work in pairs, with partner dictating the level of tension in each body part.''
- ''Select the order of body parts to be tensed.''

Student Success Goal
- 24 total shots

  6 shots while manipulating shoulder tension (2 at level 1; 2 at 5, 2 at 3)

  Repeat above sequence 4 times

To Reduce Difficulty
- Have student execute shots in ascending order of tension (1–5).
- Golfer may focus on just one body part at a time.

To Increase Difficulty
- Have partner specify level of tension in each body part of golfer.
- Specify different tensions in each body part, for instance, *5* in rear hand, *1* in target hand, and *1* in shoulders.

2. *Distraction Drill*

[Corresponds to *Golf*, Step 12, Drill 2]

Group Management and Safety Tips

- Review safety procedures.
- Use a line formation.
- Partner work is effective.

Equipment

- Golf balls, 10 per student
- Targets in the hitting area
- Clubs, 1 per student (preferably 5- or 7-iron)

Instructions to Class

- ''In golf, it is easy to be distracted by other events or thoughts. You must learn to control your thoughts and direct your attention to the swing itself.''
- ''Practice intentionally being distracted. Learn to control your response to that distraction.''

Student Option

- ''Choose the body parts to tense, the level of tension for each, and the order you use.''

Student Success Goal

- 8 total shots in the following sequence:

  2 while counting backward by 3s

  2 while reciting the alphabet backward

  2 while naming everyone in the class

  2 after using proper routine, relaxing and using a swing cue

To Reduce Difficulty

- Only make student focus on one body part at a time.

To Increase Difficulty

- Specify the level of tension and the body parts involved.
- Mix the tension levels (1-5) and body parts, and change for each shot.

3. Possibilities Drill
[Corresponds to *Golf*, Step 12, Drill 3]

Group Management and Safety Tips

- Review safety procedures.
- Use a line formation.

Equipment

- 5- or 7-iron, 1 per student
- Balls, 10 per student

Instructions to Class

- "When playing golf, it is easy to see the problems in each hole, or to doubt your abilities. Instead, practice seeing the possibilities in each hole."
- "If you see a problem and doubt your ability to conquer it, say 'Stop.' Replace any self-doubting thought with a self-enhancing one."
- "Try these examples, and then make up your own:

  a. Imagine a large water hazard and a negative thought about your ability to hit over it. Then replace it with a good thought and hit a ball over the imaginary water.

  b. Imagine landing next to a sand trap and being afraid that your next shot would land in it. Then replace that thought with a good one, and hit a ball over the trap, directly at the target.

  c. Imagine a very tight fairway, with a big dogleg. Tell yourself that "I can never make this shot," and then see yourself hitting the ball out-of-bounds, and having to play a provisional ball from the same spot. Then say "Stop," and imagine yourself saying a self-enhancing statement, and seeing the ball land in a safe area in the middle of the fairway.

  d. Make up your own potentially troublesome situation. What negative thoughts or fears do you have? Then replace those fears with positive, self-enhancing images and statements."

Student Options

- "Diagram imaginary holes and then play them."
- "Have your partner draw the holes and their strengths."

Student Success Goals

a. Replace a negative image and thoughts about a water hazard with positive thoughts and images.

b. Replace fear of hitting into a sand trap with successful thoughts.

c. Replace negative thoughts about hitting out-of-bounds with self-enhancing thoughts.

d. Replace your own negative thoughts about some situation with positive thoughts.

To Reduce Difficulty

- Describe all actual situations.
- Have partner create situations for golfer.

To Increase Difficulty

- Have student record using negative thoughts on a tape recorder. Student should then play them back and respond with new, self-enhancing thoughts.

4. Mastery and Coping Tapes Drill
[New drill]

Group Management and Safety Tips

- Prepare a handout sheet with the description of the task and two columns headed like this:

  Negative Thoughts

  Replacement Positive Thoughts

- If using tape recorders, be sure students know how to treat them and keep them out of swing range and out of danger of being hit by golf balls.

Equipment

- Paper and pencil brought by each student
- [Optional] Tape recorder and blank tape for each pair of students

Instructions to Class

- "There are often situations in golf when you can become frustrated or irritated at your performance. The important thing is not to let those negative thoughts get in the way of positive thoughts."
- "When you have a negative thought, use the thought stoppage technique to interrupt it with a trigger. Then replace it with a good, positive thought."
- "Write down 5 negative thoughts that you have had while practicing or playing golf (for example, 'I can't ever seem to hit a 5-wood straight' or 'I'm so dumb, I always rush my shots and hit slices')."
- "Then write down 5 self-enhancing, positive statements to counteract the negative ones ('I have really been practicing my 5-wood—if I take my time, I know I can hit a good shot' or 'I will use my preshot routine just the way I have been practicing it, and then I won't slice the ball, I'll hit it straight')."
- [Optional] "Now record those statements on tape with the same emotional quality as they could have occurred on the course. Play them back and listen to the more positive approach that is possible for your problems."

Student Options

- "Write down thoughts or speak into tape."
- "Work either with partner or alone."

Student Success Goal

- Create a script (or actual tape) of a series of negative thoughts, which are then countered by positive thoughts

To Reduce Difficulty

- Have student talk out loud while actually practicing, while partner writes down statements.
- Give student a tape recorder to set nearby while practicing. Student talks out loud during practice, recording anxious thoughts.

To Increase Difficulty

- Not applicable

Step 13   Course Etiquette

Golf has often been called the "sport of gentlemen" (and ladies!). Part of the beauty of golf besides the surroundings in which it is played is the way in which golfers conduct themselves. Players are responsible for their own behavior and for knowing and abiding by the rules and etiquette associated with the game. Students should be taught and encouraged to practice proper etiquette and implement rules appropriately.

STUDENT KEYS TO SUCCESS

- Quick play
- Proper order of play
- Other golfer considered first

Course Etiquette Rating

CRITERION	BEGINNING LEVEL	INTERMEDIATE LEVEL	ADVANCED LEVEL
Playing in Groups	• Tries to play in large groups	• Avoids being paired with stranger	• Enjoys new foursomes
Teeing Off	• Doesn't make reservations	• Has reservations, but shows up late	• Has tee times and keeps them
On Green	• Putts out of order • Fails to tend flag • Lays flag anywhere	• Putts in order • Fails to tend flag • Knows where to lay flag	• Putts in order • Tends flag properly
Playing Without Delay	• Slow to leave green • Slow between shots	• Putts slowly • Slow between shots	• Reads putts ahead of time
Awareness of Safety	• Hits too soon	• Watches for others	• Watches for others
Course Care	• Does not replace divots • Does not rake bunkers • Does not repair ball marks	• Replaces divots • Does not rake bunkers • Does not repair ball marks	• Replaces divots • Rakes bunkers • Repairs ball marks
Use of Cart	• Parks cart on wrong side of green	• Parks cart on wrong side of green	• Moves cart to the side near the next tee

Course Etiquette Rating

CRITERION	BEGINNING LEVEL	INTERMEDIATE LEVEL	ADVANCED LEVEL
Dress	• Wears shorts and T-shirt	• Wears shorts or skirts and sport shirt	• Wears slacks or skirt and sport shirt
Shoes	• Wears tennis shoes	• Tennis or golf shoes	• Wears golf shoes
Courtesy	• Noisy • Stands in line of other's putts	• Noisy • Stands in line of other's putts	• Quiet • Avoids lines

Error Detection and Correction for Course Etiquette

Course etiquette is important in making the game enjoyable and safe for all players. If access to a golf course is not possible, or is limited, discussions and mock situations can be set up to practice and review course etiquette. The errors below are those frequently observed by golfers. They can be discussed in your practice sessions along with other errors described in *Golf: Steps to Success*.

ERROR	CORRECTION
1. Golfer shows up to play without reserving a tee time.	1. Remind golfer that he or she should call most courses ahead of time and ask for a tee time.
2. Golfer has 10:00 tee time and arrives at the course at 9:55.	2. Golfer should be ready to tee off at the scheduled time, having already warmed up and dressed to play.

ERROR	CORRECTION
3. Golfer is in a twosome. Golfer hits first for 200 yards. Partner hits 180 yards. First golfer hits the next shot before partner.	3. The person farther from the green should hit the next shot. Therefore, the partner should hit second shot before first golfer.
4. On the green, one player's ball is 10 feet away from the hole and on the fringe, whereas partner is 20 feet away but on the green. Partner putts first.	4. To save time, all players should usually be on the green before anyone putts a ball. Player on the fringe should have hit the next shot. Once both are actually on the green, the golfer with the farther putt goes next.
5. Player hits a 20-foot putt that strikes the unattended flag and falls into the hole.	5. A putt from the green must not hit the flag. If it does, it is a 2-stroke penalty.
6. A foursome is stopped by the course ranger and reprimanded for not raking bunkers or replacing divots.	6. All golfers are expected to rake the bunkers from which they shot and to replace all divots.

Selected Course Etiquette Drills

1. *True-False Quiz Drill*
[New drill]

Equipment
- Copy of the quiz for each student
- Pencil for each student (or students provide own)

Instructions to Class
- "Golfers are expected to understand and demonstrate their knowledge of both the rules and etiquette of the game of golf."
- "Read each of the following statements and identify whether each is true or false. If the statement is false, rewrite it so that it becomes a true statement."

Student Success Goal
- 10 questions answered correctly

Quiz
- Reproduce one copy for each student.

GOLF ETIQUETTE TRUE-FALSE QUIZ

Directions: Read each statement carefully. Indicate whether it is true or false by circling the corresponding T or F. If the answer if false, rewrite the statement to make it true. To correct a statement, cross out the false part, and substitute a correct word or phrase.

T F 1. If you hit a potentially dangerous shot, you should yell "duck."

T F 2. The golfer who is farthest away from the hole always putts first.

T F 3. After all golfers have teed off, the one who hit the shortest shot will be the golfer to hit the next shot.

T F 4. If you are the first one to the green, you should always remove the flag and lay it on the fringe area.

T F 5. If 3 golfers are on the green, and one is in a sand trap, the golfer in the trap always hits before anyone else putts.

T F 6. If there is a foursome playing right behind you and they are constantly having to wait for your group to play, you should always have them "play through."

T F 7. When eight golfers show up at the course at one time, they determine tee times by drawing lots.

T F 8. It is important to replace a divot that you have taken if there is enough time.

T F 9. If your ball lands hard on the green and leaves a ball mark, you should jump on the mark a few times to flatten out the area.

T F 10. After all golfers have putted, you should gather around the flag and record your scores.

Answers to True-False Quiz

1. F Yell "fore."
2. F Only if all golfers are on the green.
3. T
4. F Only if no other player requests that the flag be tended.
5. T
6. F Only if there is room in front of you to allow them to play through.
7. F Golfers should make tee times ahead and determine own foursomes.
8. F Always replace divots.
9. F Repair ball marks by gently lifting up area with a tee, then carefully tapping down on it.
10. F Move off the green to the next tee before recording scores.

2. Fill in the Blank Drill
[New drill]

Equipment
- Copy of the quiz for each student
- Pencil for each student (or students provide own)

Instructions to the Class
- "Golfers are expected to understand and demonstrate their knowledge of both the rules and etiquette of the game of golf."
- "Read each of the following statements; provide the missing word or phrase."

Student Success Goal
- 10 questions answered correctly

Golf Etiquette Quiz
- Reproduce one copy for each student.

GOLF ETIQUETTE QUIZ

Directions: Read each question carefully, and determine the missing word or phrase. Carefully print in the missing word or phrase. (Note that the size of the blank does not necessarily correspond to the space needed to write your answer.)

1. When a foursome tees off on the first hole, the order of play is determined by _____ _____ .

2. On holes 2 through 18, the person teeing off first is said to have the _____ _____ .

3. When a partner asks you to hold the flag and remove it right after he or she has putted, you are said to be _____ .

4. If your ball lands hard on the green and makes a hole, it is said to have left _____ _____ .

5. After you hit a ball out of a bunker, you should _____ _____ .

6. Golfer A hit his ball onto the green, 1 foot from the pin. Golfer B hit her ball onto the fringe of the green, 10 feet from the pin. Golfer C hit his ball onto the green, 15 feet from the pin. Golfer _____ takes the next shot.

7. All golfers must wear _____ or _____ shoes to play golf.

8. The largest number of people who can play in one group, playing the same hole at once is _____ .

9. If you are about to putt from the green, and another golfer's ball is potentially in the way of your putt, what should you do? _____ .

10. Where should you park your cart near the green? _____ .

Answers to Quiz

1. flipping a coin
2. honors
3. tending the flag
4. a ball mark
5. rake bunker
6. B
7. golf shoes, smooth-soled shoes
8. 4
9. Ask golfer to ''mark'' his or her ball
10. On the far side of the green, near the path to the next tee

Step 14   Shot Selection and Course Management

Helping golfers learn to manage strategy during a round of golf is a very challenging task. Just like any other skill, though, course management can be practiced, and improvement will be shown. In this step the students are practicing making judgments about how to play particular golf courses or how to deal with certain types of shots. The following section can help you determine the typical problems of golfers and find ways to help them improve their play on the course.

STUDENT KEYS TO SUCCESS

- All aspects of hole considered
- Self-knowledge of strengths and weaknesses
- Personal strengths exploit hole's weaknesses
- Systematic club selection

Shot Selection and Course Management Rating

CRITERION	BEGINNING LEVEL	INTERMEDIATE LEVEL	ADVANCED LEVEL
Assessing Own Skills	• Overestimates ability to drive	• Overestimates	• Estimates properly
Identifying Strengths and Weaknesses of Hole	• Sees more trouble than safe areas • Does not consider all options • Poor at reading greens	• Afraid to be conservative • Sees more clearly • Poor at reading greens	• Accurate appraisal • Reads greens adequately
Matching Personal Strengths With Weaknesses of Hole	• Overestimates own ability • Does not consider ''LTD'' of shot	• Overestimates own ability • Does not consider ''LTD'' of shot	• Estimates ability well • Considers ''LTD''

Error Detection and Correction for Shot Selection and Course Management

As your students play on the course, they will begin to develop a better understanding of shot selection and course management. Errors in shot selection and course management are usually due to students' overestimating their strengths on the course and avoiding their weaknesses in practice. Both areas are addressed below.

ERROR

CORRECTION

1. Student always tries to hit first shot the maximum distance.

1. Depending on the hole, it may be appropriate to "lag up" to a hazard, rather than trying to hit maximum distance and hoping ball clears the water.

2. Golfer hits short on par 3 holes.

2a. Tell student not to allow the body to be too tense.

b. Remind golfer that most "trouble" on a par 3 is short of the hole. It may be safer to go beyond the hole.

3. Student sees sand traps on the right of the fairway, but still lands there.

3. Have student look for the safe landing areas. Most holes are designed to draw golfer's attention to the trouble (hole's strength). Golfer must actively look for hole weaknesses.

ERROR

CORRECTION

4. When a ball is hit from a divot, it always seems to land short of the target because of a fat shot.

4. Remind golfer to always check "LTD"—the lie, trajectory desired, and distance—before hitting. If the lie is in a divot, golfer should move the setup position slightly to the rear of center.

5. Golfer focuses on the pin on each green. Shot fails to land the ball on the green, even though there is a very large putting surface.

5. Have student analyze the strength of the hole (tight pin placement) and focus on the weakness (the large green). Then student aims at the large, open area of the green.

ERROR 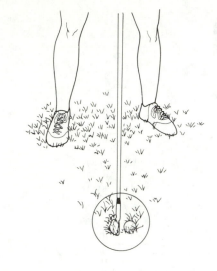	CORRECTION
6. Golfer hits shot out of high rough short of the target. 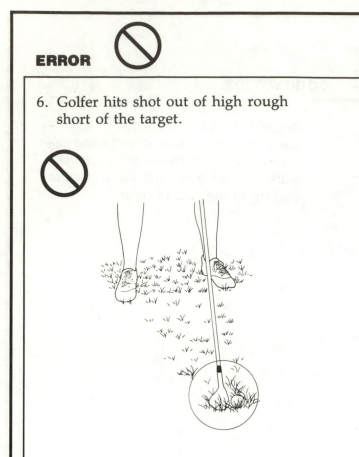	6. Grass that is cut high should be treated as a lie problem. Have student select a club designed to get out of the rough first, then worry about the distance.

Selected Shot Selection and Course Management Drills

1. Imaginary Hole
[Corresponds to *Golf*, Step 14, Drill 1]

Group Management and Safety Tips

- Review safety procedures.
- Use a line formation.
- Provide sample holes in a diagram form.

Equipment

- Golf balls, 10 per student
- Clubs, 2–3 per student (or group)
- Targets, 10–15 in the field
- Diagrams of sample holes.

Instructions to Class

- ''Being able to see the possibilities, rather than the problems, in a hole is important.''

- ''Imagine a golf hole in the practice area. Identify the strengths and the weaknesses of the hole, with corresponding safe landing areas.''
- ''Pretend the flags and targets in the field are trouble spots, strengths of the hole. Those trouble spots always draw attention.''
- ''The key is to be able to find the safe landing areas in spite of the trouble. Imagine a hole, then find 10 safe landing areas.''
- ''Hit 1 shot to each of those safe areas. You may use different clubs. Keep track of the clubs used and whether you landed in the safe areas.''

Student Options

- "Identify strengths of the hole and safe landing areas."
- "Work with partner to alternate shots and determine strengths and weaknesses of holes."

Student Success Goal

- 8 of 10 shots hit to safe landing areas

To Reduce Difficulty

- Provide layouts of holes, with targets set in practice field corresponding to the strengths of the holes.
- Let student work with partner, so they identify strengths and weaknesses together.

To Increase Difficulty

- Have student draw holes and indicate safe landing areas before hitting.
- Put more targets in the field.

2. *Alternate Strategies*
[Corresponds to *Golf*, Step 14, Drill 2]

Group Management and Safety Tips

- This is a good indoor or rainy day activity.
- Have multiple examples of golf holes available.

Equipment

- Paper and pencil for each student
- Prepared diagram of a golf hole(s), 1 or more per student

Instructions to Class

- "Each golfer has different strengths and weaknesses. Because of the specific characteristics of the golfer, each might choose to play a hole with a different strategy."
- "Assume you are each of the following golfers. How would you play the hole that I have diagramed?"

Student Option

- "Select multiple routes for each golfer."

Student Success Goal

- Given a specific golf hole, select a route and club for each type of golfer

  Long hitter with good short game

  Short hitter who tends to slice

  Student (describe self)

To Reduce Difficulty

- Provide relatively simple holes.
- Let student work with partner.

To Increase Difficulty

- Provide diagrams of complex golf holes.
- Provide more detailed characteristics of each golfer for student to take into account.

3. *Listing Strengths and Weaknesses*
[Corresponds to *Golf*, Step 14, Drill 3]

Group Management and Safety Tips

- This is a good indoor or rainy day activity.
- Provide multiple layouts of holes.

Equipment

- Pencil for each student
- Set of diagrams for each student

Instructions to Class

- "On any golf hole, there are several strategy options. In order to choose the optimal strategy, identify all the strengths and weaknesses first. Then decide how to play the hole."
- "For each of the holes listed, identify at least 3 strengths and 3 weaknesses (desired landing areas) for that hole."

Student Options

- "Select optional routes."
- "Choose partners."
- "You may choose from among the several types of holes I have diagramed."

Student Success Goal

- List at least 3 strengths and 3 weaknesses for each hole

To Reduce Difficulty

- Provide diagrams of holes that are rather uncomplicated.
- Let golfer work with partner.

To Increase Difficulty

- Provide more complex holes.
- Have partner help evaluate student's choices.

4. *Managing an Entire Hole*
[Corresponds to *Golf*, Step 14, Drill 4]

Group Management and Safety Tips

- Distribute multiple hole layouts.
- If there is a "home course," be sure to use some of its holes for diagram.
- After students analyze holes, discuss options.
- There will be a wide variety of club selection due to individual differences, however, your perceptions of student strengths and weaknesses may differ from the students'.
- Use this drill for individual feedback.

Equipment

- Pencils, 1 per student
- Handouts with diagrams of an entire 18-hole course

Instructions to Class

- "When you are ready to play, it is a good idea to consider how you will play each hole."
- "Using the diagrams that were distributed, mark the landing spot for each of your shots. Over each landing area, indicate the club you would use."

Student Options

- "Identify the weaknesses in each hole."
- "Select route and club for each shot."

Student Success Goal

- Plot all shots for each hole and indicate the clubs to be used by placing abbreviations on the diagram

To Reduce Difficulty

- Provide simple diagrams, with holes possessing few strengths.
- Let student work with partner

To Increase Difficulty

- Provide more complex course layouts.
- Have partner judge the first student's hypothetical shot of each hole, then redefine where the ball lands. The student "golfing" must then plot a new strategy to finish the hole.

Answers for Example Hole Weaknesses

[Corresponds to *Golf*, Step 14, Drill 4, Diagrams a, b, c]

a. Hole *a*'s weaknesses
   1. Wide landing area off tee
   2. Few hazards
   3. Open landing area to right of green
   4. Large green

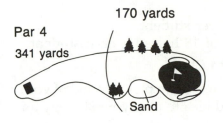

b. Hole *b*'s weaknesses
   1. No hazard on backside of green
   2. Open landing area in front of green
   3. Large green
   4. Short yardage for Par 3

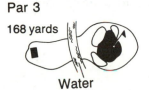

c. Hole *c*'s weaknesses
   1. Short yardage for Par 5
   2. Safe landing areas all along right side of fairway
   3. Large landing areas
   4. No hazard in front of green
   5. Large green

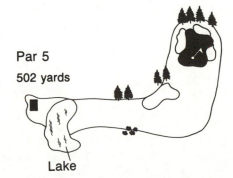

5. Managing a Round
[Corresponds to *Golf*, Step 14, Drill 5]

Group Management and Safety Tips

- Provide multiple course layouts of varying degrees of challenge.
- Students may work in pairs.

Equipment

- Pencils, 1 per student
- Diagrams of 18 holes for each student

Instructions to Class

- ''When planning to play a round of golf, it is a good idea to plan your strategy for each hole.''
- ''On the diagram, show the safe landing areas you have chosen and the club you will hit from each area. Be sure to consider both the strengths and weaknesses of each hole.''

Student Options

- ''Select desired routes and clubs.''
- ''Choose the course you want out of the selection of layouts I have provided.''

Student Success Goal

- Plot course management for each of the 18 holes

To Reduce Difficulty

- Provide sample holes that are relatively simple and free of trouble.
- Let student work with a partner.

To Increase Difficulty

- Provide more complex course layouts.
- Have student complete task in a fixed amount of time.

6. *Actual Course Play*
[New drill]

Group Management and Safety Tips

- Arrange for course use and tee times two weeks in advance and confirm in writing, if possible.
- Prepare foursomes and tee-off times two days before course play and post. When possible play an experienced player in each group or invite experienced players to join your class for the first time on a course.
- Review safety procedures.
- Encourage fast play. A suggestion for speeding up play would be to limit each player to a total of 10 strokes on each hole, then move on to the next hole.

Equipment

- Sample scorecard and/or diagram of the course to be played
- Pencils, 1 per student
- Golf balls, 4 good golf balls per student (have students supply their own and/or extra balls)
- Set of golf clubs with bag, 1 per student (or have students supply own)

Instructions to Class

- "You will be playing a round of golf."
- "To prepare for the round, study the course layout."
  [*Note*: Instructor provides layout of the course to be played.]
- "Determine your strategy for playing each hole. Remember to identify the strengths and weaknesses of each hole. Then match them with your own skills. Diagram the shots you will attempt to hit in each situation."
- "Remember, when you actually play, the only shot you can totally predetermine is the tee shot. From then on, you need to respond based on where your last shot landed and on the LTD for the next shot."

Student Option

- "You choose course management for each hole, including clubs selected and landing spots identified."

Student Success Goal

- Actually play an 18-hole course after having decided on course management

To Reduce Difficulty

- Discuss each hole with the class.

To Increase Difficulty

- Not applicable

Step 15 Learning From Your Round of Golf

Playing a round of golf should give each student many opportunities to test skills in a "real" golf setting. The results of all the hours of practice will now have an opportunity to be tested on the course, with all of its challenges and frustrations. One of these challenges is learning from the results of shots hit during a round of golf.

Step 15 describes several techniques for learning from a round of golf. Just like a basketball player might have someone chart his or her shots, a golfer should keep track of shots—the circumstances under which they are hit and the results. Using a Shotkeeper or diagraming shots on the course are two good ways the student can learn from a round and use that experience to direct future practice.

STUDENT KEYS TO SUCCESS

- Self-monitoring is critical
- Self-monitoring is habitual
- Self-monitoring of both physical and mental aspects
- Learns from ball flight

Learning From Round Rating

CRITERION	BEGINNING LEVEL	INTERMEDIATE LEVEL	ADVANCED LEVEL
Ability to Learn From Ball Flight	• Minimal	• Moderate	• Good
Physical Aspects **Clubface and Path Errors**	• Sometimes observes path and face errors	• Sees path and face errors	• Adjusts for path and face errors
Alignment	• Must focus on it	• Becomes part of routine	• Part of routine
Swing Techniques	• Needs outside observer to detect	• Can detect some gross errors	• Detects from changes in the feeling of swing or result
Mental Techniques **Mental Errors**	• Unlikely to remember mental errors	• Begins to focus on mental skills	• Sensitive to importance of mental skills
Use of Routine	• Seldom monitored	• Becomes more important	• Very important
Positive Thinking	• Difficult after errors	• Begins to use for all shots	• Uses thought stoppage and positive self-talk
Tension Control	• Monitors in hands only	• Monitors in hands and shoulders	• Monitors and controls in all body parts

Error Detection and Correction for Learning From Rounds of Golf

The consequences of shot selection become more vivid on the course. The charting drills will help you and the students to more objectively identify errors in shot selection and course management that are often overlooked if relying on memory alone.

ERROR

CORRECTION

1. Golfer fails to record results of each shot.

1. Tell student to make it a habit to record results of each shot as the club is returned to the bag.

2. Golfer has a good idea of the physical problems with the swing, but no idea of mental aspects.

2a. Have student record at least one mental aspect for each shot.

  b. Have golfer play a round, focusing only on mental aspects.

3. Golfer uses diagram method of plotting shots, but is unable to draw generalizations from the diagrams.

3a. Have student make a table with every club listed. Write down the characteristics of each shot hit with each club.

  b. Golfer could use the Shotkeeper as a method of summarizing what was diagramed.

4. Tony, the golfer in the Shotkeeper example, does not identify his tendencies or use them to establish practice strategies (see the Sample Shotkeeper Scorecard, which corresponds to Figure 15.3 in *Golf: Steps to Success*).

4. Sit down with Tony and review the card. Note the following:
   - Good job in pitching
   - Good control with 5-wood
   - Good job on second putts
   - Compare control of 5-wood with that of 3-wood
   - Failure to use routine and learn from the results

Sample Shotkeeper Scorecard

Name Tony Jones Course Richmont CC Date Sept. 9

Performance Chart

Hole	Yards	PAR	Woods 1	2	3	4	5	Irons 4	5	6	7	8	9	Wedge	Greens hit in Regulation	Putts 1st	2nd	3rd
1	385	4			S / BT				S / BT		S / BT			L / BT		u / CC	✓ / CC	
2	142	3						R / FR					✓ / FR	✓ / CC		o / FR	u / FR	✓ / CC
3	501	5			R / FR		✓ / CC		L / FR				✓ / FR			u / BT	✓ / CC	✓ / FR
4	365	4			S / BT		R / FR						L / FR	✓ / FR		u / BT	o / FR	✓ / CC
5	325	4			R / FR		R / FR		✓		o / FR		L / FR			✓ / BT	✓ / CC	✓ / FR
6	129	3					h / FR		L / FR		o / FR		L / FR	✓ / CC	✓	u / BT	✓ / FR	✓ / BT
7	498	5			S / BT		✓ / FR		L / FR		L / FR		L / FR			u / BT	✓ / BT	
8	301	4			S / BT		✓ / FR		S / BT		L / FR			✓ / CC		✓ / BT	✓ / BT	
9	379	4						R / FR	R / FR		L / FR			✓ / CC		u / FR	✓ / CC	
10	516	5			S / BT		✓ / CC	R / FR	L / FR					✓ / BT		o / CC	✓ / CC	
11	329	4			S / BT		✓ / CC	R / FR	R / FR					✓ / BT		u / BT	✓ / FR	
12	145	3					✓ / CC	R / FR					L / FR	✓ / CC		✓ / CC	✓ / CC	
13	371	4			R / FR		✓ / CC		L / FR				L / FR	✓ / BT		✓ / BT	✓ / CC	
14	298	4					✓ / CC		R / FR					✓ / CC		✓ / CC	✓ / CC	
15	520	5					✓ / CC		R / FR				u / FR	✓ / CC		o / FR	✓ / FR	
16	318	4			S / BT				R / FR					✓ / FR	✓	o / FR	✓ / CC	
17	141	3						✓ / CC								✓ / CC	✓ / CC	
18	352	4					✓ / UA		R / BT				o / FR	o / FR		u / FR	✓ / CC	

Physical Aspects
✓ = on target
s = sliced
h = hooked
o = beyond target
u = short of target
r = right of target
l = left of target

Mental Aspects
NT = Negative Thinking
LA = Lack of Attentional Control
BT = Excess Body Tension
FR = Failure to use Routine
OA = Overaroused
UA = Underaroused
CC = Complete Mental Control

Summary:

Physical Aspects		Mental Aspects	
✓ = 43	o = 8	NT = —	OA = —
s = 9	u = 12	LA = —	UA = 1
h = 1	r = 12	BT = 24	CC = 28
	l = 11	FR = 42	

Selected Learning From Round of Golf Drills

1. *Using Shotkeeper From Practice Tee*
[Corresponds with *Golf*, Step 15, Drill 1]

Group Management and Safety Tips

- This is a good partner activity.
- This is a good indoor or rainy day activity.

Equipment

- Handout diagrams of 6 golf holes (copies for every student)
- Pencils, 1 per student (or students supply own)
- Blank Shotkeeper Scorecards, 1 per student

Instructions to Class

- "It is very important to learn from every round of golf you play."
- "The Shotkeeper Scorecard is designed so that you can record both physical and mental characteristics associated with each shot."
- "Look at the scorecard, and note the way in which you record each shot's physical characteristics:

  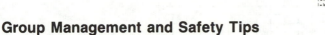 = on target
  s = sliced
  h = hooked
  o = over or beyond target
  u = under or short of target
  r = right of target
  l = left of target."

- "Now look at the mental characteristics that are important:

  NT = negative thinking
  LA = lack of attentional control
  BT = excess body tension

  FR = failure to use routine
  OA = overaroused
  UA = underaroused
  CC = complete mental control."

- "In order to practice using this card, imagine that you are playing the 6 holes diagramed on the handout."
- "Select a club for each shot and imagine how you would hit the shot. Record one physical and one mental aspect."

Student Options

- "Select club to use for each shot."
- "Diagram holes of your own design."
- "Work with a partner and code for each other."

Student Success Goal

- Pretend to play the 6 holes diagramed, using the Shotkeeper Scorecard and recording each club used and the physical and mental aspects of each shot

To Reduce Difficulty

- Only make student focus on either physical or mental aspects, not both.
- Provide descriptions of a golfer's behavior and have students code it.
- Demonstrate shots and have students code them. Talk out loud so they can record your mental aspects.

To Increase Difficulty

- Make holes more difficult.
- Have student actually hit the shots and record reactions.

2. *Plotting Holes*
[Corresponds to *Golf*, Step 15, Drill 2]

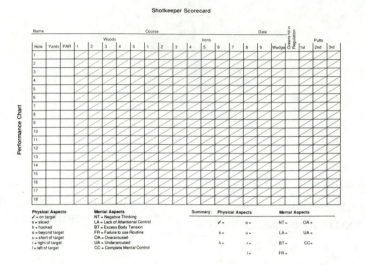

Shotkeeper Scorecard

Group Management and Safety Tips

- Encourage students to play on own time (outside of class).
- Remind students of safety, rules, and etiquette for course.
- Walk around with various foursomes.

Equipment

- Shotkeeper Scorecards, 1 per student
- Sets of clubs, 1 per student (or group)
- Access to play 6 holes of golf
- Golf balls, 4 per student (or students bring their own)

Instructions to Class

- "The assignment for our next class is to play 6 holes of golf."
- "On each shot, be sure to record three elements: (a) the club used, (b) a physical characteristic of the resulting shot, and (c) a mental characteristic that describes you during or just before you hit the shot."

Student Options

- "Choose which club to use for each shot."
- "Record element for physical and mental aspects."

Student Success Goal

- 6 holes of golf, noting at least one physical aspect and one mental aspect of each shot

To Reduce Difficulty

- Only make student focus on either physical or mental aspects, not both.
- Have student play fewer holes.
- Have partner record physical aspects of golfer.

To Increase Difficulty

- Increase number of holes played and analyze each.

3. *Organizing Practice Drill*
[Corresponds to *Golf*, Step 15, Drill 3]

Equipment

- Paper and pencil for each student (or students supply own)
- Students must bring their completed Shotkeeper Scorecard from Drill 2

Instructions to Class

- "Review your Shotkeeper Scorecard for the 6 holes you played."
- "Look at each club one at a time and decide whether you have any predictable problem or bias. Look at all the clubs, and see if there is a common pattern."
- "Tally the number of mental problems you had. Are there any patterns?"
- "Select two of the areas identified. Make a commitment to practice them."
- "It helps to review the drills used in Steps 1 through 14 and select ones to match the problem."

Student Success Goals

- Based on the Shotkeeper recorded in Drill 2, select two aspects of game to practice, decide how to practice each aspect (including doing a drill), and list them below:

  a. "I need to practice _____ .

  Therefore, I will do _____

  drill _____ times."

  b. "I need to practice _____ .

  Therefore, I will do _____

  drill _____ times."

Step 16   Setting Goals for Continued Success

In order for your students to continue to make progress in their golf skills, it is important for them to help keep track of their strengths and weaknesses, using such techniques as the Shotkeeper Scorecard (see Step 15). The student can then link problems with drills that help them practice the correct techniques (see Steps 1–14).

In this step, you guide them as they select and state their goals for future skill development. Each goal should be determined by the student in terms of the strengths and weaknesses that are demonstrated in practice and during a round of golf. Be sure that the goals meet the criteria of being achievable, measurable, realistic, stated in positive terms, and formulated with target dates.

STUDENT KEYS TO SUCCESS

- Goals based on strengths and weaknesses
- Commitment to written goals
- Goals characterized as
    achievable,
    measurable,
    realistic,
    positive, and
    time-constrained

Goal-Setting Rating

CRITERION	BEGINNING LEVEL	INTERMEDIATE LEVEL	ADVANCED LEVEL
Based on Golfer's Strengths and Weaknesses	• Not well identified	• Moderately well identified	• Clearly identified
Stated in Achievable Terms	• Not realistic (over-estimates)	• Moderately realistic	• Realistic
Stated in Measurable Terms	• General terms (e.g., ''get better'')	• Attaches terms that are measurable	• Well done
Stated in Realistic Terms	• Not believable	• Believable	• Believable
Stated Positively	• Stated in negative terms (e.g., ''don't bogey'')	• More positive statements	• Very positive statements
Defined in Terms of Time	• Generalizations	• Time limits specified	• Time limits specified

Error Detection and Correction for Goal Setting

Your students will tend to write goals that are not specific relative to the stated criteria. The Success Goals provided with each drill can be used as a review for goal setting. The errors below are commonly observed in goal setting.

Writing goals may be a new experience for many students. Some students will respond to the process in a more positive manner than others. Setting goals is often intimidating for students because of their fear of failure.

ERROR

CORRECTION

1. You write goals for your student.

1a. Goals must be individualized, written by the student.

  b. You should review goals to be sure they meet criteria.

2. Goals are not based on realistic judgments of strengths and weaknesses.

2. Have student use analysis techniques such as Shotkeeper Scorecard to record actual mental and physical skills.

3. Goals are too long-range and do not focus attention on structured practice.

3. Have golfer establish long-term goals, then work backward to set short-term goals related to daily or weekly practice.

4. Goals are not stated clearly, nor do they meet the criteria. The following examples represent weak goals, with the corresponding corrections representing a better goal statement:

4. Have student clearly state goals in ways that meet criteria.

Weak Statement

a. I want to improve my putting by taking 20 putts per day.

  (This needs to be more specific and time-constrained.)

b. For the next 5 days, I will practice only my 4-iron.

  (Generally, student should practice the weak area between strong ones.)

c. I will not talk negatively to myself during this round of golf.

  (Student should add positive thoughts.)

Stronger Statement

a. I will practice 20 putts per day—5 at 3 feet, 5 at 4 feet, 5 at 5 feet, and 5 at 6 feet—for the next 10 days.

b. I will start each practice for the next 5 days with ten 5-iron shots, followed by thirty 4-iron shots, and ending with ten 3-iron shots.

c. Each time I have a negative thought, I will use thought stoppage, then replace it with a positive one.

Selected Goal-Setting Drills

1. *Identifying Areas for Improvement Drill*
[Corresponds to *Golf*, Step 16, Drill 1]

Group Management and Safety Tips

- This is a good indoor activity.
- Partners work well.

Equipment

- Students bring completed Shotkeeper
- Pencils, 1 per student (or students supply own)

Instructions to Class

- "It is important to be able to identify your strengths and weaknesses objectively."
- "Use the Shotkeeper Scorecard that you completed when you played a full 9 holes. Look down the column corresponding to each of the clubs you used. Analyze your tendencies."

Student Options

- "Analyze areas for improvement."
- "Write out comments from your Shotkeeper Scorecard."

Student Success Goal

- 9 holes of golf, using the Shotkeeper Scorecard to record physical and mental aspects of shots, analyzing overall strengths and weaknesses, and selecting one element for improvement in each of the following categories:

  Woods

  Long irons

  Middle irons

  Short irons

  Chipping

  Pitching

  Putting

  Sand play

  Uneven lies

To Reduce Difficulty

- Let student work with partner, helping each other identify strengths and weaknesses.
- Allow golfer to select only one or two clubs to analyze.
- Specify which clubs to analyze.

To Increase Difficulty

- Require golfer to list both physical and mental aspects.
- Have students analyze each other's cards.

2. Goal-Setting Drill

[Corresponds to *Golf*, Step 16, Drill 2]

Group Management and Safety Tips

- This is a good indoor activity.
- Partners work well.

Equipment

- Pencils, 1 per student (or students supply own)
- List of characteristics of hypothetical golfers

Instructions to Class

- "Once you have identified your strengths and weaknesses, it is important to be able to focus attention on areas for improvement."
- "Assume you have the characteristics of this golfer" [state those listed previously].
- "Write 1 goal statement for each area. Be sure to use the criteria we discussed regarding a good goal statement:

  Achievable

  Realistic and specific

  Measurable

  Time-constrained."

Student Options

- "Write goal statements."
- "Work in pairs."
- "Make up other sets of golfer characteristics."

Student Success Goal

- 4 well-stated goals based on the following characteristics:

  a. 3 of 4 tee shots were sliced

  b. the routine was not used 12 times

  c. 2 of 3 shots with the 9-irons did not go high into the air

  d. 7 of 9 first putts were short of the hole

To Reduce Difficulty

- Make characteristic lists very obvious.
- Let student work with partner to help check goal statements.
- Have student use own characteristics.

To Increase Difficulty

- Have student write sets of characteristics.
- Make golfer write both physical and mental goals.
- Require student to write both long-term and short-term goals.

3. Future Improvement Identification Drill

[Corresponds to *Golf*, Step 16, Drill 3]

Future Improvement Targets for Golf

Name _____   Date _____

For each of the clubs listed below, identify the typical characteristics you see in the ball flight coming from each kind of club. Use the same abbreviations used in the Shotkeeper Scorecard and describe each characteristic in terms of the number of times out of 10 that something happened, for example, Driver: 7 of 10 slices.

Woods: Driver 　　　　3- or 5-Wood	
Long Irons: 1–3	
Middle Irons: 4–6	
Short Irons: 7–9	
Pitching Wedge	
Sand Wedge	
Putting	

Group Management and Safety Tips

- This is a good indoor activity.
- Partners work well.

Equipment

- Students bring own Shotkeeper Scorecard
- Future Improvement Targets Cards, 1 per student (students supply own)
- Pencils (or students supply own)

Instructions to Class

- "After you have identified your tendencies by using the Shotkeeper, you must translate that information into a plan for future improvement."
- "Think about your strengths and weaknesses for the following clubs:

  Woods

  Long irons

  Middle irons

  Short irons

  Pitching wedge

  Sand wedge

  Putter."

- "Write one statement to describe your tendencies with each club. State the tendencies in terms of the number of times out of 10 in which something happened (e.g., 7 out of 10 times, . . .).
  Note: If you hit 2 of 4 shots, that would be stated as '5 of 10.' "
- "Use the same abbreviations that you used on your Shotkeeper."

Student Options

- "Interpret Shotkeeper data."
- "Work with a partner."

Student Success Goal

- Using the Shotkeeper Scorecard as a source of information, write a future improvement target for each club or group of clubs

To Reduce Difficulty

- Have students state problems in true numbers rather than converting to base 10.
- Let student work with partner.

To Increase Difficulty

- Have golfer identify weaknesses, and also use them as bases for goal statements.

4. *Goal Achievement Card Drill*

[Corresponds to *Golf*, Step 16, Drill 4]

Goal Achievement Card

Name _____   Date _____

Skill	Specific Goal	Practice Strategy	Target Date
Example Putting	Putt 7 of 10 balls into hole from 5 feet	Cluster Putting Drill 5 times Ladder Drill 5 times Line Drill 5 times	April 5
1 Long Irons or Woods			
2 Middle Irons			
3 Short Irons			
4 Chipping and Pitching			
5 Putting			

Group Management and Safety Tips

- This is a good indoor activity.
- Have students work with partners to help check goal statements.
- Make a list of problems and corresponding drill options.

Equipment

- Goal Achievement Cards, 1 per student (students supply own)
- Pencils (or have students supply own)

Instructions to Class

- "Once you have identified your strengths and weaknesses, it is important to write goals and convert them into operational directions or practice strategies."
- "Using the Goal Achievement Card, write 5 specific goals."
- "Then think back over all the drills we have used, or refer to your book. Choose at least one drill to help you attain each goal."

Student Options

- "Select areas for improvement."
- "Select and write goals."
- "Select appropriate drills."
- "Work in pairs."

Student Success Goal

- 5 specific goals set, and a practice strategy and target date determined for each

To Reduce Difficulty

- Let student use goals written previously.
- Provide list of problems and specific drills that are found in Step 4 of the instructor's book.

To Increase Difficulty

- Have students remember drills without using book.
- Make golfer state 5 physical and 5 mental goals.

Evaluation Ideas

A strong educational program must incorporate evaluation techniques from the very beginning. The evaluation procedures you implement should directly reflect the educational objectives that you hold for the golf unit. If the objectives include developing basic skills and knowledge related to golf, along with the social skills, appreciation for the history of golf, and understanding of golf equipment, then the evaluation scheme should include all of those elements.

The objectives of your golf unit should be shared with the class on the first day. At the same time, you should distribute and discuss the evaluation process you plan to implement. One example of a set of general objectives is the following:

- To develop the personal skills (at the beginning level) necessary to comfortably and enjoyably play the game of golf;
- To understand and demonstrate the rules, strategy, safety, and etiquette of each activity; and
- To demonstrate the ability to analyze the fundamental skills required for the game of golf.

Whatever evaluation process you decide upon, it should provide for reliable and valid assessments of the knowledge and skills your students have acquired during the golf unit. In order to enhance this aspect and provide for efficient use of time, it is important to determine testing procedures that match the maturation of your students and the nature of your unit.

TESTING PROCEDURES

Many golf units employ both objective skill tests and written knowledge tests. The skill tests may include both technique and performance measures covering all of the skills taught in the unit or selected from among the more important beginning skills. When deciding on a strategy for the administration of the skill tests, you may wish to consider the following aspects:

- Format and inclusive nature of the tests;
- Scheduling of the tests; and
- Administration of evaluation techniques.

FORMAT OF THE TEST

One good technique for evaluation is to utilize standardized skill tests to determine the product or performance aspects of the skill. For example, determining how far and accurately a student can hit a golf ball with a 5-iron can be an excellent skill test. However, it may be equally important in terms of your objectives to determine the process or "style" of the golf swing, as determined by the ability to demonstrate the elements of the Keys to Success, or the checklist provided for each skill.

It is not necessarily appropriate to attempt to test all of the physical skills that you have taught. For example, it is possible that due to facilities, you may have merely introduced such skills as sand shots, uneven lies, or shot selection on the golf course. There is no reason why these concepts cannot be tested cognitively, even if they are not tested in terms of physical demonstration.

SCHEDULING OF THE TEST

Beginning golfers tend to learn golf skills at various rates. For that reason, it may be wise to schedule skill tests at various times during the unit. For example, if your philosophy includes criterion levels of learning and self-paced progress, you may wish to give all skill tests on three or four occasions during the unit. Students could be allowed to take the tests as many times as they wish and count the best score only. Or your philosophy may require "performance on demand," in which case you may wish to hold only one testing session for each skill.

Similar strategies could be used for written knowledge tests. You may wish to structure one examination or a series of examinations. Our preference would be to structure the examinations to match the learning environment and philosophy of your teaching. The important element is to be sure that skill tests and written examinations match the objectives established for the class.

ADMINISTRATION OF THE EVALUATION PROCEDURES

If your basic philosophy has been one that includes a great deal of student involvement, your evaluation procedures may also reflect that philosophy. For example, it is very possible for students to work in partners, trios, or foursomes and test each other. For younger students, objective tests can be structured so that the students score each other's performances, and help in the logistics of testing. If the level of maturation of the students is sufficient, they can also be involved in evaluating the process or techniques involved in golf. After all, part of the objectives of this unit included students becoming familiar with checklists and learning to utilize them reliably. If that has been accomplished, then they could certainly be involved in the evaluation process.

One effective technique for evaluation is to distribute a list of skill competencies on the first day of class. These competencies can be provided in many different formats, including the objectives listed at the end of this section or a sheet of competencies such as those that follow:

Grip, Stance, and Swing: Demonstrate the appropriate grip, stance, and swing for the following shot patterns: hook, slice, and straight. Place the date and the tester's initials under each element when it is demonstrated:

	Grip	Stance	Swing
Hook			
Slice			
Straight			

Chipping: Demonstrate the ability to chip a ball, from 20 yards, into an area with an 86-inch radius (the length of 2 standard drivers) around the cup.

(#) _____ out of 10 attempts; date _____ ; tester _____ (8 = A; 7 = B; 6 = C; 5 = D; 4 or less is not satisfactory)

Course Play: Demonstrate the ability to play a round of 9 holes at _____ golf course. Record your score, counting all strokes taken plus any penalty strokes.

(55 or less = A; 56–60 = B; 61–65 = C; 66–71 = D; more than 71 strokes on 9 holes is not satisfactory)

Another way to communicate your expectations as a teacher is to provide a list of technical and performance objectives that provides a suitable list of evaluation criteria. For example, if the pitch shot is thought to be 10% of the content to be covered in this class, 5% in terms of technique and 5% in terms of performance, then 10% of the evaluation should be based on that skill plus its concomitant knowledges. Each of the objectives that you state for your class must be capable of being evaluated. If you state the objectives in behavioral terms, these can in fact become the basis for your evaluation scheme. See Appendix D.1, "Sample Individual Program," for specific examples of technique and performance objectives.

Test Bank

The following test questions have been compiled from *Golf: Steps to Success*. Select questions as they fit your needs.

WRITTEN EXAMINATION QUESTIONS

Directions: Select the *one best* answer for each question.

1. What was the country of origin of the game of golf as it is known today?
   a. Greece
   b. England
   c. Scotland
   d. United States

2. What is one of the biggest problems in playing golf?
   a. physical skills
   b. mental control
   c. trying too hard
   d. lack of strength

3. Where was the first golf club in the United States founded?
   a. Massachusetts
   b. New York
   c. Connecticut
   d. Pennsylvania

4. Course terms: Select the appropriate definition for each term.

Terms	Definitions
_____ Lateral water hazard	a. Perimeter of a course
_____ Dogleg	b. Water hazard crossing the fairway
_____ Hole	c. Starting point for each golf hole
_____ Tee	d. Water hazard parallel to the fairway
_____ Fairway	e. Ending point of playing a hole
_____ Out-of-bounds	f. Central path from tee to green
_____ Direct water hazard	g. Curve in design of hole
	h. Highest cut grass

Rules: Questions 5–11 are situations arising during play requiring rulings.

5. Betty and John are playing the 5th hole, a par 5. John is unsure of what club to hit and asks Susie for assistance. What is the ruling?
   a. no penalty
   b. 1-stroke penalty
   c. 2-stroke penalty
   d. disqualification

6. John is walking in the trap. He trips and his club hits the sand. What is the ruling?

   a. no penalty
   b. 1-stroke penalty
   c. 2-stroke penalty
   d. disqualification

7. Pete chipped his third shot onto the green; it hit the pin and went into the hole. What was his score on this hole?

   a. 3
   b. 4
   c. 5
   d. 6

8. Betty hit her fourth shot into a sand trap. The ball landed in an area of accumulated water. She dropped her ball in the trap, hit her next shot onto the green, and 3-putted. What was her score on the hole?

   a. 9
   b. 7
   c. 10
   d. 8

9. Pete is playing a par 3 hole. He lost his ball on his tee shot and hit the next ball into the hole. What was his score on the hole?

   a. 1
   b. 2
   c. 3
   d. 4

10. John hit his third shot into a lateral water hazard. He hit his next shot onto the green and 2-putted. What was his score on the hole?

    a. 7
    b. 6
    c. 6
    d. 8

11. Susie is playing the 4th hole, 329 yards, par 4. She hit her tee shot out-of-bounds, the next shot in the fairway. She whiffed the following shot. The next shot went on the green and she made her putt. What was her score?

    a. 5
    b. 6
    c. 4
    d. 7

12. Cardiovascular endurance is a major factor in preparing your body for golf success.

    a. True
    b. False

13. Golf requires more strength development than flexibility.

    a. True
    b. False

14. Which exercise is not for flexibility?

    a. head rotation
    b. arm across chest
    c. walking
    d. forearm rotation

15. Club terms: Match the lettered parts on the club with the corresponding term.

    ____ Hosel
    ____ Grooves
    ____ Sole
    ____ Face
    ____ Toe
    ____ Shaft

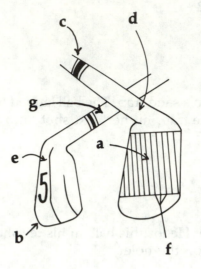

16. Which club is used the *most* in golf?

    a. driver
    b. 5-iron
    c. putter
    d. sand wedge

17. Which club is the *longest*?

    a. 5-iron
    b. 3-iron
    c. 4-iron
    d. 6-iron

18. Which club results in the *greatest* distance?

    a. 5-iron
    b. 7-iron
    c. 4-iron
    d. 9-iron

19. Which club results in the *highest* trajectory?

    a. 9-iron
    b. 5-iron
    c. sand wedge
    d. pitching wedge

20. Which club has the *least* loft?

    a. putter
    b. driver
    c. 3-wood
    d. 9-iron

21. What is the maximum number of clubs a player may have in a set?
    a. 13
    b. 15
    c. 14
    d. 12

Scoring: Refer to the scorecard for questions 22–27:

Hole	1	2	3	4	5	6	7	8	9	Total
Yardage	320	150	480	350	130	354	520	319	296	2,919
Par	4	3	5	4	3	4	5	4	4	36
Susie	6	3	7	3	1	4	6	6	4	40
John	6	4	6	5	3	4	4	5	3	40
Betty	4	2	6	8	4	4	5	6	2	41
Pete	5	3	5	4	4	4	5	4	5	39

22. On which hole did Betty score a double bogey?
    a. 4
    b. 8
    c. 5
    d. 9

23. Who scored the first birdie?
    a. Susie
    b. John
    c. Betty
    d. Pete

24. Who scored the first bogey?
    a. Susie
    b. John
    c. Betty
    d. Pete

25. Who scored par on the 3rd hole?
    a. Susie
    b. John
    c. Betty
    d. Pete

26. Who had an eagle on the 9th hole?
    a. Susie
    b. John
    c. Betty
    d. Pete

27. On which hole did Susie have an ace?
    a. 2
    b. 7
    c. 4
    d. 5

28. What is the designated standard of excellence in golf?

    a. eagle
    b. birdie
    c. par
    d. bogey

29. In the setup position, how is the weight distributed on the feet?

    a. heels to midstep
    b. midstep
    c. midstep to balls of feet
    d. balls of feet

30. Where is the ball position for the full swing with woods?

    a. near the center
    b. toward the target heel
    c. toward the rear heel
    d. varies with the wood

31. Where is the ball position for the full swing with irons?

    a. near the center
    b. toward the target heel
    c. toward the rear heel
    d. varies with the iron

32. In which direction do the Vs of the target and rear hands point?

    a. toward the rear shoulder
    b. toward the rear side of the chin
    c. toward the chin
    d. toward the target side of the chin

33. In which hand is the club gripped more in the fingers?

    a. target hand
    b. rear hand

34. What is the warning cry in golf?

    a. ''Turn!''
    b. ''Fore!''
    c. ''Down!''
    d. ''Duck!''

35. Which is not considered good course etiquette?

    a. raking traps
    b. replacing divots
    c. repairing ball marks
    d. removing stakes

36. After the completion of the hole, when is the score marked on your scorecard?

    a. before leaving the green
    b. on the next tee
    c. just off the green
    d. as players finish putting

37. Which ball is played first in a foursome *after* the tee shot?

 a. ball closest to the hole
 b. ball farthest from the hole
 c. ball in the rough
 d. ball farthest from the green

38. Who is the "official" when playing golf?

 a. USGA
 b. RAGA
 c. the players as a group
 d. the individual player

39. What initiates the full swing backswing?

 a. hands
 b. arms
 c. arms, hands, club
 d. shoulders, arms, hands, club

40. What initiates the full swing forwardswing?

 a. arms
 b. target heel and arms
 c. upper body
 d. hips

41. Which best describes the setup position of the chip shot?

 a. weight even, alignment square (shoulders, hips, feet)
 b. weight target side, alignment square (shoulders) and open (feet, hips)
 c. weight even, alignment open
 d. weight target side, alignment open

42. Which best describes the setup position for the pitch shot?

 a. weight even, alignment square
 b. weight target side, alignment square (shoulders) and open (hips, feet)
 c. weight even, alignment open
 d. weight target side, alignment open

43. Which shot can be best described as having minimum trajectory and maximum roll?

 a. sand
 b. putt
 c. pitch
 d. chip

44. Which shot can be best described as having maximum trajectory and minimum roll?

 a. putt
 b. pitch
 c. chip
 d. sand

45. If you hit a ball into the sand, what is your first consideration?

 a. club selection
 b. trajectory needed
 c. distance to the pin
 d. lie of the ball

46. With shots close to the green, which is the higher percentage shot?

    a. pitch
    b. chip

47. What swing length best describes the full swing?

    a. 1-to-1
    b. 3-to-3
    c. 5-to-5
    d. 6-to-6

48. What swing lengths best describe the pitch shot?

    a. 2-to-2, 3-to-3
    b. 4-to-4, 5-to-5
    c. 3-to-3, 4-to-4
    d. varies from 2-to-2 through 4-to-4

49. What other setup position most resembles the setup for the buried lie shot?

    a. pitch shot setup
    b. chip shot setup
    c. full swing setup
    d. uneven lie, ball above the feet setup

50. What has the greatest influence on the curvature of ball flight?

    a. grip
    b. clubface at contact
    c. alignment
    d. shoulder alignment at contact

51. What is the major factor to consider when reading greens?

    a. distance to the hole
    b. type of grass
    c. dry and wet conditions
    d. slope of the green

52. What has the greatest influence on the initial direction of the ball?

    a. path of the club at contact
    b. alignment of the blade
    c. body alignment
    d. clubface at contact

53. If your ball flight consistently starts to the right of your target, what is the first thing you should check?

    a. path of the club at impact
    b. alignment of the blade
    c. alignment
    d. clubface at impact

54. If you consistently top shots or hit shots thin, what should you check first to correct this?

    a. grip
    b. posture
    c. alignment
    d. width of stance

Ball flight: Refer to the diagram for questions 55–57.

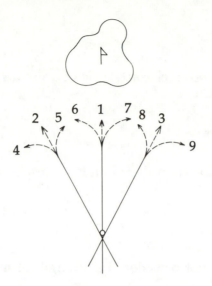

55. For a right-handed golfer, which ball flight combination best illustrates a push-slice?
    a. 4
    b. 5
    c. 8
    d. 9

56. For a left-handed golfer, which ball flight combination best illustrates a pull-hook.
    a. 4
    b. 5
    c. 8
    d. 9

57. Which ball flight combination is ideal?
    a. 6
    b. 1
    c. 2
    d. 7

58. Given these four golfers, who have each teed off on a par 3 hole, who hits next?
    a. golfer A, 20 feet from the hole and in the sand trap
    b. golfer B, 25 feet away and on the fringe of the green
    c. golfer C, 30 feet from the pin and on the green
    d. golfer D, 20 feet from the pin and on the green

59. What is the optimal level of tension in the hands?
    a. 5
    b. 3
    c. 4
    d. 10

60. What is a trigger in thought stoppage?

    a. the grip on the club
    b. your first finger
    c. any interrupting signal
    d. yelling "fore"

61. Which of the following is not a characteristic of a good goal?

    a. achievable
    b. target-dated
    c. assigned by the teacher
    d. measurable

62. What do golfers tend to do when their hands are especially tight or tense?

    a. hook
    b. slice
    c. birdie
    d. pull

63. Which of the following is not considered a strength of a hole?

    a. out-of-bounds
    b. a large green
    c. a narrow fairway
    d. many hazards

64. Which of the following should you analyze first when you walk up to your ball in the fairway?

    a. distance from green
    b. club to be used
    c. lie of the ball
    d. trajectory needed for the shot

65. Where is the ball positioned in the stance when playing uphill or downhill lies?

    a. center
    b. close to the low foot
    c. close to the high foot
    d. varies with the woods and irons

66. What is the ball flight tendency in playing a shot off a sidehill lie with the ball below the feet?

    a. straight
    b. slice
    c. hook
    d. push

67. What is a major focus in playing uneven lies?

    a. swing length
    b. swing pace
    c. direction
    d. balance

68. When do you first assess your strengths and weaknesses as a player?

    a. playing the course
    b. during practice
    c. after a round
    d. on the tee

69. What is the first step in tension control?

    a. to make a tight fist and relax
    b. to take a deep breath
    c. to make a "3" in your neck and shoulders
    d. to exhale and breath in

70. What is one of the most important aspects of your preshot routine?

    a. distance to target
    b. setup
    c. self-monitoring
    d. selection of target

71. What ball flight results from a grip pressure of "2"?

    a. hook
    b. slice
    c. pull
    d. push

72. Which is *not* a hole's strength?

    a. high rough
    b. wide fairway
    c. lateral water hazard
    d. trees and shrubs

73. You have hit your third shot to within 10 feet of the green. How do you determine your next shot?

    a. consider success from practice
    b. consider distance to the pin and trajectory needed
    c. consider lie of the ball, distance to the pin and trajectory needed
    d. consider lie of the ball and distance to the pin

74. You have hit your tee shot into the woods on the fourth hole. What should you do?

    a. Drop another ball on the tee with no penalty.
    b. Play a ball from where you think the other ball went into the woods with one stroke penalty.
    c. Play a provisional ball from the tee in case you can't find your original tee shot.
    d. Play a provisional ball with a one stroke penalty and don't look for your original tee shot.

75. Susie is 15 yards from the green with a trap between the ball and the green. The pin is 20 feet from the fringe. Which club is most appropriate for Susie's next shot?

    a. 7-iron
    b. 5-iron
    c. 9-iron
    d. PW

76. You have used the Shotkeeper Scorecard for two 18-hole rounds. In tallying the physical characteristics, you note that you consistently slice and push the ball. What should you check first in your practice session as a possible cause for the slice and push ball flight on the golf course?

    a. grip position
    b. alignment
    c. grip pressure
    d. stance

77. Betty is on the eighth hole and preparing to hit her fourth shot over a water hazard. As she is taking her setup, she begins to think about her shot going into the water. What should she do?

   a. Hit the shot. The thought is normal when hitting over a hazard.
   b. Stop the thought by changing clubs and hit the shot.
   c. Stop the negative thought by thinking positive thoughts, then hit the shot.
   d. Stop the negative thought by thinking positive thoughts then change clubs and hit the shot.

78. You are practicing the full swing with a 5-iron and continuously top the ball. Which one of the following drills should you practice?

   a. wide whoosher drill
   b. one-leg toe drill
   c. cocking drill
   d. one bucket drill

79. Evaluate the following goal statement:
   "I will dedicate myself to become a better sand shot player and putter by May 15."

   a. meets one criteria
   b. meets two criteria
   c. meets three criteria
   d. meets four criteria

80. You are buying a set of golf clubs. Which of the following best describes the club characteristics you need to consider when purchasing clubs?

   a. lie, loft, grip size, and length
   b. weight, loft, grip size, and length
   c. weight, lie, length, and grip size
   d. weight, loft, and grip size

ANSWERS TO WRITTEN EVALUATION QUESTIONS

1. c	16. c	42. a	68. b
2. c	17. b	43. d	69. b
3. b	18. c	44. b	70. d
4. d	19. c	45. d	71. a
g	20. a	46. b	72. b
e	21. c	47. c	73. c
c	22. b	48. c	74. c
f	23. c	49. b	75. d
a	24. d	50. b	76. b
b	25. d	51. d	77. c
5. c	26. c	52. a	78. b
6. c	27. d	53. c	79. a
7. a	28. c	54. b	80. c
8. d	29. c	55. d	
9. c	30. b	56. d	
10. a	31. a	57. b	
11. b	32. b	58. b	
12. b	33. b	59. b	
13. b	34. b	60. c	
14. c	35. d	61. c	
15. d	36. b	62. b	
f	37. b	63. b	
e	38. d	64. c	
a	39. c	65. c	
b	40. b	66. b	
g	41. b	67. d	

Appendices

Appendix A

How to Use the Knowledge Structure Overview

A knowledge structure is an instructional tool—by completing one you make a very personal statement about what you know about a subject and how that knowledge guides your decisions in teaching and coaching. The knowledge structure for golf outlined here has been designed for a teaching environment, with teaching progressions that emphasize technique and performance objectives in realistic settings. In a coaching environment, you would need to emphasize more physiological and conditioning factors, with training progressions that prepare athletes for competition.

The Knowledge Structure of Golf shows the first page or an *overview* of a completed knowledge structure. The knowlege structure is divided into broad categories of information that are used for all of the participant and instructor guides in the Steps to Success Activity Series. Those categories are:

- physiological training and conditioning,
- background knowledge,
- psychomotor skills and tactics, and
- psycho-social concepts.

Physiological training and conditioning has several subcategories, including warm-up and cool-down. Research in exercise physiology and the medical sciences has demonstrated the importance of warming up before and cooling down after physical activity. The participant and instructor guides present principles and exercises for effective warm-up and cool-down, which, because of time restrictions are usually the only training activities done in the teaching environment. In a more intense coaching environment, additional categories should be added—training principles, injury prevention, training progressions, and nutrition.

The background-knowledge category outlines subcategories of essential background knowledge that all instructors should have mastery of when beginning a class. For golf, background knowledge includes playing the game of golf, basic rules, golf today, and equipment.

Under psychomotor skills and tactics, all the individual skills in an activity are named. For golf, these are shown as full swing motion, setup, applying full swing motion with irons/woods, ball flight, pitching, chipping, putting, sand, and uneven lies. These skills are also presented in a recommended order of presentation. In a completed knowledge structure, each skill is broken down into subskills, delineating selected technical, biomechanical, motor learning, and other teaching and coaching points that describe mature performance. These points can be found in the Keys to Success and the Keys to Success Checklists in the participant book.

Once individual skills are identified and analyzed, selected basic tactics of the activity are presented and analyzed. For golf these are identified as effective practice, pre-shot routines, etiquette, shot selection and course management, learning from a round, and setting goals.

The psycho-social category identifies selected concepts from the sport psychology and sociology literature that have been shown to contribute to learner's understanding of and success in the activity. These concepts are built into the key concepts and the activities for teaching. For golf, the concept identified is preparing for a round: mental skill.

To be a successful teacher or coach, you must convert what you have learned as a student or done as a player or performer to knowledge that is conscious and appropriate for presentation to others. A knowledge structure is a tool designed to help you with this transition and to speed your *steps to success*. You should view a knowledge structure as the most basic level of teaching knowledge you possess for a sport or activity. For more information on how to develop your own knowledge structure, see the textbook that accompanies this series, *Instructional Design for Teaching Physical Activities*.

Knowledge Structure of Golf (Overview)

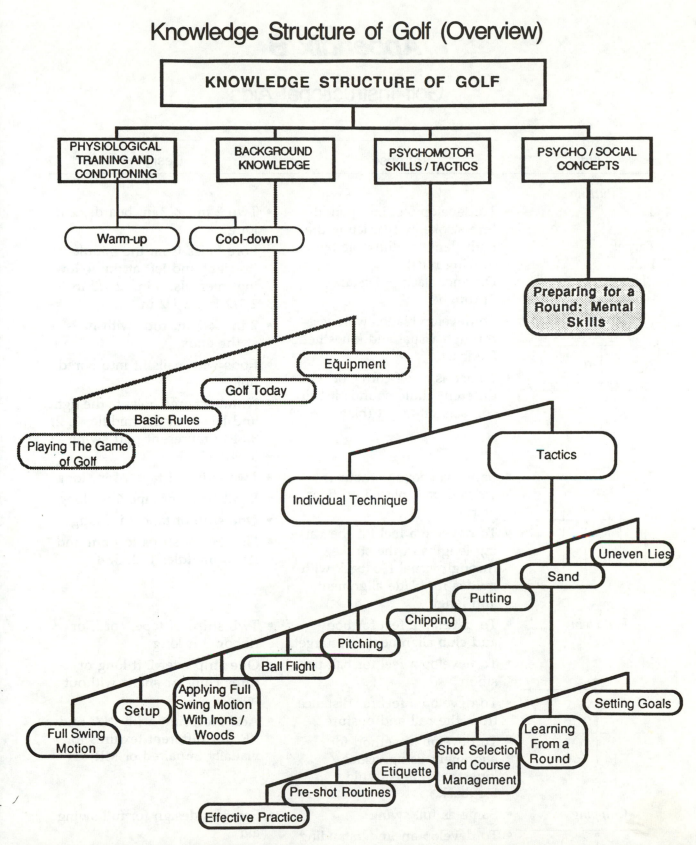

Note. From "The Role of Expert Knowledge Structures in an Instructional Design Model for Physical Education" by J.N. Vickers, 1983, *Journal of Teaching in Physical Education*, **2**(3), pp. 25, 27. Copyright 1983 by Joan N. Vickers. Adapted by permission. This Knowledge Structure of Golf was designed specifically for the Steps to Success Activity Series by Joan N. Vickers, Judy P. Wright, DeDe Owens, and Linda K. Bunker.

Appendix B

Golf Instructional Aids

Aid	Purpose	Design
Putting		
1. Target Ball Blade	• To develop feel in a pendulum stroke by restricting the path (length adjustable by moving rods) Distance Back = Distance Through • To develop blade awareness through visual and kinesthetic feedback • To act as a self-corrector with different audio sounds if ball contacts off-target (blade error)	• Two 2 in. × 2 in. boards, 2 ft long • Bore holes from the middle (to right and left at the following intervals: 3 in., 2 1/2 in., 2 1/2 in., 2 1/2 in. • 2 in. × 7 in. rods with nails at the ends • Rods with nails fit into bored hole • Number bored holes to the right and left from the middle: 1, 2, 3, 4 to represent putt swing lengths
2.	• Same as above without restricted path placed on floor or rug • To develop a feel for the varying lengths in the stroke, through visual feedback with guides for blade alignment and length	• Two strips of tape 24 in. long • Eight strips of tape 6 in. long • One strip of tape 8 in. long • Number of strips to right and left of middle: 1, 2, 3, 4
Full swing	• To develop a feel for body and club alignment to a target • To develop a feel for ball position • To develop a feel for distance from the ball and posture • To develop a method for alignment using visual, kinesthetic, and tactile feedback	• Two strips of tape, cord, or ribbon 3 ft long • One strip over 2 ft long or three clubs or shafts without heads • Add footprints with ''L'' and ''R'' or different textures for visually impaired or MR
Chipping	• Same as full swing • To develop an understanding and feel for the differences in posture and positioning in the short shot and full swing	• Same as design for full swing aid

Posture
Platform designs

1.

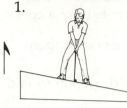

- To develop a feeling of maintaining the swing center during the swing
- To develop an understanding of posture and weight changes for specialty shots (up-, down-, and sidehill) using visual and kinesthetic feedback

- 3 1/2 ft square heavy plywood with ends 2 in. and 6 1/2 in. high
- Rubber matting cover with a brush mat attachment for left- and right-handed golfers. It should be stable enough to hit balls from

2.

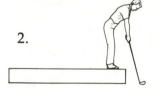

- To develop a feeling of free arm hand, posture, and swing center at address using visual and kinesthetic feedback

- 3 ft square heavy plywood 6 in. high

Indoor wall targets

1.

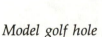

- To develop an understanding of club loft and trajectory through visual, kinesthetic, and audio feedback, and audio feedback with adaptation

- Line 2 ft above the floor

2.

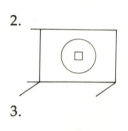

- To develop target awareness with club loft and trajectory (circle in square may reinforce academic work of MRs and young children)

- Place tape at centerpoint on a wall, make circle 3 ft diameter, square 9 ft width

3.

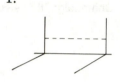

- To provide self-testing and motivation in practice

- Same design as above, with an additional circle with a 12 ft diameter
- Audio adaptations: Use contrasting sound coverings for each area

Model golf hole

- To develop an understanding of hold design and terminology using visual and tactile feedback

- 1 ft × 2 in. plywood
- Three contrasting surfaces for rough, fairway, green, and tee
- 30 toothpicks: 10 yellow around direct hazard, 10 red around lateral hazard, and 10 white on side for out-of-bounds
- Bore out traps and hazards for real sand and water
- Braille lettering of terms

Ball-club contact

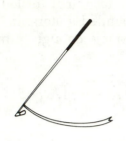

- To develop swing motion with ball-club contact using visual, kinesthetic, and audio feedback

- L-shaped rod mounted on a platform that can be stabilized either in- or outdoors. Suspend a plastic ball by a cord.

Arm and hand speed

- To develop an understanding of arm and hand speed relative to acceleration and effects of centrifugal force using visual, kinesthetic, and audio feedback
- To show effective use of centrifugal force, as the streamers or ribbons stay out in an arc
- To provide a swishing sound with clubhead speed

- Crepe streamers or ribbons 6 ft long
- Tie streamer or ribbon to end of club

Note. From *Teaching Golf to Special Populations* (pp. 157-160) by D. Owens (Ed.), 1984, Champaign, IL: Leisure Press. Copyright 1984 by Leisure Press. Adapted by permission.

Appendix C.1

Sample Scope and Teaching Sequence

NAME OF ACTIVITY: Golf

LEVEL OF LEARNER: _____

Legend: New [N]   Review [R]   Continue [C]   Student Directed Practice** [P]

Steps	Session Number	1	2	3	4	5	6	7	8	9	10	11	12	13	14	15	16	17	18	19	20	21	22	23	24	25	26	27	28	29	30
1	Introduction *	N																													
1	Full swing motion	N	R	R	R	R	R	R	R	R	R	R	R	R	R	P	P	P	P	P	P	P	P	P	P	P	P	P			
2	Setup		N	R	R	R	R	R	R	R	R	R	R	R	R	P	P	P	P	P	P	P	P	P	P	P	P	P			
3	Full swing with clubs			N	C	R	R	R	R	R	R	R	R	R	R	P	P	P	P	P	P	P	P	P	P	P	P	P			
4	Ball flight						N	R	R	R	R	R	R	R	R	P	P	P	P	P	P	P	P	P	P	P	P	P			
5	Pitching								N	R	R	R	R	R	R	P	P	P	P	P	P	P	P	P	P	P	P	P			
6	Chipping											N	C	R	R	R	R	P	P	P	P	P	P	P	P	P	P	P			
7	Putting													N	C	R	R	R	P	P	P	P	P	P	P	P	P	P			
8	Sand shots															N	R	R	P	P	P	P	P	P	P	P	P	P			
9	Uneven lies																	N	R	R	P	P	P	P	P	P	P	P			
10	Effective practice															N	R	R	R	R	R	P	P	P	P	P	P	P			
11	Routines													N	R	C	R	R	P	P	P	P	P	P	P	P	P	P			
12	Mental skills																N	R	C	R	R	P	P	P	P	P	P	P			
13	Etiquette			N															R	C	R	R	P	P	P	P	P	P			
14	Course management																		N	R	R	R	P	P	P	P	P	P			
15	Learning from round																			N	R	P	P	P	P	P	P	P			
16	Setting goals																					N	P	P	P	P	P	P			
17	Quiz			▓																											
18	Exam																												N		
19																															
20																															
21																															
22																															
23																															
24																															

RAINY DAY FROM DAY 4 - 27

Notes: *Warmups done every day.

**Students have directed practice on their own in stations each day.

Appendix C.2
How to Use the Scope and Teaching Sequence Form

A completed Scope and Teaching Sequence is, in effect, a master lesson plan. It lists all the individual skills to be included in your course, recorded (vertically) in the progressive sequence in which you have decided to present them and showing (horizontally) the manner and the sessions in which you teach them.

The Sample Scope and Teaching Sequence (Appendix C.1) illustrates how the chart is to be used. This chart indicates that in session 3, the class will review skills presented in Steps 1 and 2, and will continue practicing the full swing with clubs. It also indicates that the skills in Step 8, for example, are worked on for three sessions—one introduction, one student directed practice, and one review.

A course Scope and Teaching Sequence chart (use the blank form in Appendix C.2) will help you to better plan your daily teaching strategies (see Appendix E.1). It will take some experience to predict accurately how much material you can cover in each session, but by completing a plan like this, you can compare your progress to your plan and revise the plan to better fit the next class.

The chart will also help you tailor the amount of material to the length of time you have to teach it. Be sure that your course's Scope and Teaching Sequence allots ample time for review and practice of each area.

Appendix C.2

Scope and Teaching Sequence

Steps	**Session Number**	1	2	3	4	5	6	7	8	9	10	11	12	13	14	15	16	17	18	19	20	21	22	23	24	25	26	27	28	29	30
1																																
2																																
3																																
4																																
5																																
6																																
7																																
8																																
9																																
10																																
11																																
12																																
13																																
14																																
15																																
16																																
17																																
18																																
19																																
20																																
21																																
22																																
23																																
24																																
25																																

New **N**   Review **R**   Continue **C**   Student Directed Practice **P**

NAME OF ACTIVITY _____

LEVEL OF LEARNER _____

Note. From Badminton: A Structures of Knowledge Approach (pp. 60, 61) by J.N. Vickers and D. Brecht, 1987, Calgary, AB: University Printing Services. Copyright 1987 by Joan N. Vickers. Adapted by permission.

Appendix D.1

Sample Individual Program

INDIVIDUAL COURSE IN _____   GRADE/COURSE SECTION _____

STUDENT'S NAME _____   STUDENT ID # _____

I. DEMONSTRATED BY PHYSICAL SKILLS

TECHNIQUE AND PERFORMANCE OBJECTIVES	WT* x	POINT PROGRESS**			= FINAL SCORE***
		1	2	3	4	
Full Swing						
Technique: Number out of 10 demonstrating 75% or more of the items on the checklist.	10%	3	4	5	6+	
Performance: Number out of 10 hit from a tee with an iron of choice. A minimum of 125 yards in length with a maximum of 25 yards off target at final resting point.	10%	3	4	5	6+	
Pitch						
Technique: Number out of 10 demonstrating 75% or more items on checklist.	5%	3	4	5	6+	
Performance: Number out of 10 hit from 40 yards away into an area with 6 yard radius using a 9-iron, PW or SW.	5%	3	4	5	6+	
Chip						
Technique: Number out of 10 demonstrating 80% or more items on checklist.	5%	5	6	7	8+	
Performance: Number out of 10 hit from 20 yards into an area with 4 yard radius with a 7-, 8- or 9-iron.	5%	4	5	6	7+	
Putt						
Technique: Number out of 10 demonstrating 80% or more items on checklist.	5%	5	6	7	8+	
Performance: Number out of 10 hit into cup from 3 feet away.	5%	4	5	6	7+	
Sand Shot						
Technique: Number out of 10 demonstrating 75% or more items on checklist.	2%	3	4	5	6+	
Performance: Number out of 10 hit out of sand from 35 yards away into an area with a 10 yard radius with a SW.	2%	3	4	5	6+	
Uneven Lies						
Technique: Number out of 10 demonstrating 75% or more items on checklist.	2%	3	4	5	6+	
Performance: Select 1 of 4 uneven lies. Number out of 10 hit in the direction of the target.	2%	3	4	5	6+	

Shot Selection and Course Management	Technique: Effectively plan 80% of shots for 4 holes on a golf course.	1.5%	5	6	7	8+
Use of Routine	Technique: Number out of 10 demonstrating routine in order of items on checklist.	2.5%	5	6	7	8+
	Performance: Number of routines out of 10 with proper sequence and alignment.	2.5%	5	6	7	8+
Attentional Control	Technique: Number out of 10 demonstrating full attention to pre-shot routine and execution.	1.5%	5	6	7	8+

SUBTOTAL PHYSICAL SKILLS = 66%

II. DEMONSTRATED BY COGNITIVE MEANS

Goal Setting	Performance: Number out of 10 goals written that meet the checklist criteria.	5%	5	6	7	8+
Etiquette	Performance: Number out of 10 correct answers on questions regarding etiquette.	8%	6	7	8	9+
Rules	Performance: Number out of 10 correct answers on questions regarding golf rules.	8%	6	7	8	9+
Mental Control	Performance: Number out of 10 examples of thought stoppage including self-enhancing statement substitutions.	5%	5	6	7	8+
Mechanics of Golf Swing	Performance: Number out of 10 correct answers on questions regarding techniques (mechanics) of golf swing.	8%	5	6	7	8+

SUBTOTAL COGNITIVE = 34%

TOTAL = 100%

*WT = Weighting of an objective's degree of difficulty.

**PROGRESS = Ongoing success, which may be expressed in terms of (a) accumulated points (1, 2, 3, 4); (b) grades (D, C, B, A); (c) symbols (merit, bronze, silver, gold); (d) unsatisfactory/satisfactory; and others as desired.

***FINAL SCORE equals WT times PROGRESS.

Appendix D.2

Individual Program

INDIVIDUAL COURSE IN _____   GRADE/COURSE SECTION _____

STUDENT'S NAME _____   STUDENT ID # _____

SKILLS/CONCEPTS	TECHNIQUE AND PERFORMANCE OBJECTIVES	WT* ×	POINT PROGRESS** =				FINAL SCORE***
			1	2	3	4	

*WT = Weighting of an objective's degree of difficulty.

**PROGRESS = Ongoing success, which may be expressed in terms of (a) accumulated points (1, 2, 3, 4); (b) grades (D, C, B, A); (c) symbols (merit, bronze, silver, gold); (d) unsatisfactory/satisfactory; and others as desired.

***FINAL SCORE equals WT times PROGRESS.

Appendix D.2
How to Use the Individual Program Form

To complete an individual program for each student, you must first make five decisions about evaluation:

1. How many skills or concepts can you or should you evaluate, considering the number of students and the time available? The larger your classes and the shorter your class length, the fewer objectives you will be able to use.
2. What specific quantitative or qualitative criteria will you use to evaluate specific skills? See the Sample Individual Program in Appendix D.2 for ideas.
3. What relative weight is to be assigned to each specific skill, considering its importance in the course and the amount of practice time available?
4. What type of grading system do you wish to use? Will you use letters (A, B, C, D), satisfactory/unsatisfactory, a number or point system (1, 2, 3, etc.), or percentages? Or, you may prefer a system of achievement levels such as colors (red, white, blue), creatures (birdies, eagles, buzzards), or medallions (gold, silver, bronze).
5. Who will do the evaluating? You may want to delegate certain quantitative evaluations to be made by the students' peers up to a predetermined skill level (e.g., a ''B'' grade), with all qualitative evaluations and all top-grade determinations being made by you.

Once you have made these decisions, draw up an evaluation sheet (using the blank form in Appendix D.2) that will fit the majority of your class members. Then decide whether you will establish a minimum level as a passing/failing point. Calculate the minimum passing score and the maximum attainable score, and divide the difference into as many grade categories as you wish. If you use an achievement-level system, assign a numerical value to each level for your calculations.

The blank Individual Program form, as shown in Appendix D.2, is intended not to be used verbatim (although you may do so if you wish), but rather to suggest ideas that you can use, adapt, and integrate with your own ideas to tailor your program to you and your students.

Make copies of your program evaluation system to hand out to each student at your first class meeting, and be prepared to make modifications for those who need special consideration. Such modifications could be changing the weight assigned to particular skills for certain students, or substituting some skills for others, or varying the criteria used for evaluating selected students. Thus, individual differences can be recognized within your class.

You, the instructor, have the freedom to make the decisions about evaluating your students. Be creative. The best teachers always are.

Appendix E.1

Sample Lesson Plan

Lesson plan _____3_____ of _____ Activity _____Golf_____

Class ___Beginner_____

Objectives:

1. Introduce safety rules: Students will demonstrate safety awareness by following the safety rules.
2. Review full swing motion without a club: (a) Students will demonstrate the arm swing, body turn, and weight shift of a swing without the club 8 of 15 times when rotated by partner checklist; (b) students will demonstrate the proper setup position 8 of 15 times when rated by partner checklist.
3. Introduce full swing motion with irons: Students will demonstrate the full swing with an iron 5 times, with a minimum of 50% of the items from the checklist exhibited.

Skill or concept	Learning activity	Teaching points	Time (min)
1. Outline objectives of class.			
2. Discuss safety rules.	• Distribute handout. • Show poster on wall.	• Each day, check equipment for damages prior to use and following class. • Emphasize potential dangers and personal responsibility.	
3. Review full swing motion.	• Redemonstrate full swing motion. • Students stand in semicircle formation.	• Review major cues: Posture Arms relaxed and hanging Target knee to rear knee Rear knee to target knee Thumbs away from target Thumbs toward target Feel body turn around the spine Visualize head as "hub of wheel"	
4. Students practice swing 15 times.	• Practice swings.	• Walk around and comment on elements of the checklist.	
5. Practice with partners, 10 swings.	• Partners use checklist for motion and setup.	• Remind students of elements of the checklist.	

6. Review setup with club.	• Redemonstrate setup.
	• Students stand in semicircle formation, first individually and then with partners.
	• Partners use checklist.
		• Discuss safety: No swinging of clubs.
		• Review major cues:
		  Grip: neutral position, Vs point to rear side of chin
		  Posture: ready position, weight midstep to balls of feet, alignment square
		  Ball position center
		  Arms hanging freely from shoulders

7. Introduce full swing with 7- or 9-iron.	• Demonstrate or use shot videotape (Sybervision Geiberger, or Sheehan).
	• Practice Wide Whoosher Drill.
		• Explain elements of full swing with iron:
		  Same swing for men and women
		  Swing fluidly
		  Arms swing and body follows
		  Wide arc equal on back- and forwardswings
		  Create motion
		    Body turn
		    Weight shift
		  Feel target arm acceleration

8. Practice 15 swings.	• Students stand in semicircle with rear shoulder to inside of circle. • Use partners.	• Place thumbs away from and toward target. • Listen to whooshing sound. • Partner uses checklist.
9. Practice 10 swings and switch.	• Practice target alignment using alignment club, student, and target.	• Emphasize the importance of target alignment by using a club on ground as alignment and setup each time. • Emphasize target awareness, not accuracy.

10. Discuss safety rules.	• Use question and answer format.	• Explain rules:
		  Full motion focus
		  Begin and end on signal
		  Enter and leave area to rear, never to side
		  Finish hitting, then move back out of space
		  Pick up all balls

11. Practice hitting full swings (25 balls each).

- Students stand in straight line with 4 yd between each hitter, 3–4 hitters per target.
- Practice the Cocking Drill, the One-Leg Toe Drill, and hitting from tees.

- Make 2 practice swings between each ball hit.
- Alternate three drill repetitions and three regular swings.

12. Use partner checklist.

- Focus on one aspect of swing at a time.

- Make sure there is enough room between stations to observe front view of students.
- Expand stations to 8 yd between each hitter.

13. Review questions, bridge to next lesson.

Appendix E.2
How to Use the Lesson Plan Form

All teachers have learned in their training that lesson plans are vital to good teaching. This is a commonly accepted axiom, but there are many variations in the form that lesson plans can take.

An effective lesson plan sets forth the objectives to be attained or attempted during the session. If there is no objective, then there is no reason for teaching, and no basis for judging whether the teaching is effective.

Once you have named your objectives, list specific activities that will lead to attaining each. Every activity must be described in detail—what will take place and in what order, and how the class will be organized for the optimum learning situation. Record key words or phrases as focal points as well as, particularly in golf, brief reminders of the applicable safety precautions (see Appendix E.1).

Finally, set a time schedule that allocates a segment of the lesson for each activity to guide you in keeping to your plan. It is wise to also include in your lesson plan a list of all the teaching and safety equipment you will need, as well as a reminder to check for availability and location of the equipment before class.

An organized, professional approach to teaching requires preparing daily lesson plans. Each lesson plan provides you with an effective overview of your intended instruction and a means to evaluate it when class is over. Having lesson plans on file allows someone else to teach in your absence. You may modify the blank Lesson Plan form shown in Appendix E.2 to fit your own needs.

Lesson Plan

LESSON PLAN _____ OF _____   OBJECTIVES:

ACTIVITY _____

CLASS _____

SKILL OR CONCEPT	LEARNING ACTIVITIES	TEACHING POINTS	TIME

Appendix F

Putting Checklist

Name: _____   Date: _____

Front View: Preswing

1. Stance	Narrower than shoulders	☐ 1
	Shoulder width	☐ 2
	Wider than shoulders	☐ 3
2. Ball position	Rear side of center	☐ 1
	Center	☐ 2
	Target side of center	☐ 3
3. Arms and hands	Rear side of ball	☐ 1
	Center	☐ 2
	Target side of center	☐ 3
4. Head position	Rear side of center	☐ 1
	Center	☐ 2
	Target side of center	☐ 3

Front View: In-Swing

5. Levers	1 (no wrists)	☐ 1
	2 (wrists)	☐ 2
6. Head position	Stationary	☐ 1
	Moves	☐ 2

Down the Line: Preswing

7. Blade	Open	☐ 1
	Square	☐ 2
	Closed	☐ 3
8. Feet	Open	☐ 1
	Square	☐ 2
	Closed	☐ 3
9. Hips	Open	☐ 1
	Square	☐ 2
	Closed	☐ 3
10. Shoulders	Open	☐ 1
	Square	☐ 2
	Closed	☐ 3
11. Eye line	Inside target line	☐ 1
	Over target line	☐ 2
	Outside target line	☐ 3
12. Body posture	Sitting back	☐ 1
	Over ball	☐ 2
	Upright	☐ 3

Down the Line: In-Swing

13. Backswing path	Inside	☐ 1
	Square	☐ 2
	Outside	☐ 3
14. Forwardswing path	Inside	☐ 1
	Square	☐ 2
	Outside	☐ 3

Appendix G

Shotkeeper Scorecard

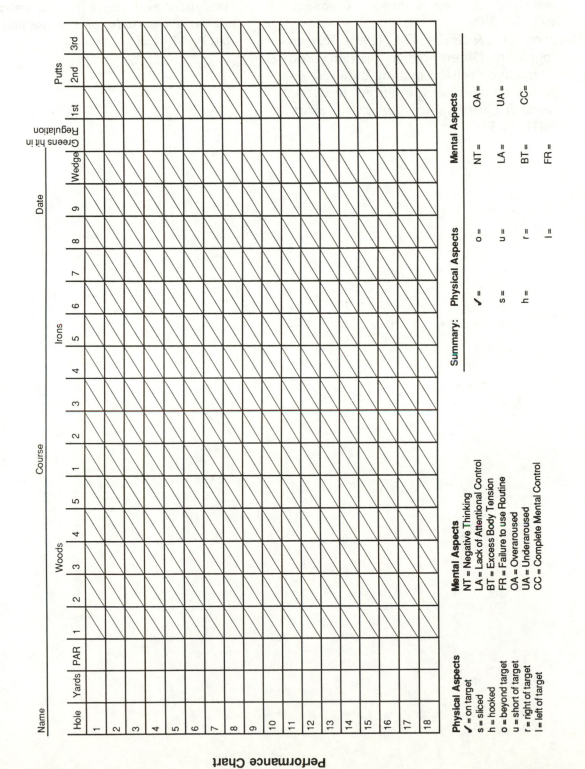

Shotkeeper Scorecard

Name _____ Course _____ Date _____

Physical Aspects

✔ = on target
s = sliced
h = hooked
o = beyond target
u = short of target
r = right of target
l = left of target

Mental Aspects

NT = Negative Thinking
LA = Lack of Attentional Control
BT = Excess Body Tension
FR = Failure to use Routine
OA = Overaroused
UA = Underaroused
CC = Complete Mental Control

Summary:	Physical Aspects		Mental Aspects	
	✔ =	o =	NT =	OA =
	s =	u =	LA =	UA =
	h =	r =	BT =	CC=
		l =	FR =	

Performance Chart

References

Goc-Karp, G., & Zakrajsek, D.B. (1987). Planning for learning: Theory into practice. *Journal of Teaching in Physical Education,* **6**(4), 377-392.

Housner, L.D., & Griffey, D.C. (1985). Teacher cognition: Differences in planning and interactive decision making between experienced and inexperienced teachers. *Research Quarterly for Exercise and Sport,* **56**(1), 45-53.

Imwold, C.H., & Hoffman, S.J. (1983). Visual recognition of a gymnastic skill by experienced and inexperienced instructors. *Research Quarterly for Exercise and Sport,* **54**(2), 149-155.

Suggested References

Books and Periodicals

Bunker, L., & Owens, D. (1984). *Golf: Better practice for better play*. Champaign, IL: Leisure Press/Human Kinetics.

Cochran, A., & Stobbs, J. (1968). *The search for the perfect swing*. London: Lippincott.

Dey, J. (1986). *Golf rules in pictures*. New York: Grosset and Dunlap.

Gallaway, T. (1981). *The inner game of golf*. New York: Random House.

Hogan, C. (1986). *5 days to golfing excellence*. Lake Oswego, OR: Merl Miller.

Jobe, F., & Moynes, D. (1986). *30 exercises for better golf*. Commerce, CA: Champion Press.

Johnson, C., & Johnstone, A. (1975). *A positive approach to golf*. New York: Random House.

Jones, E. (1986). *Swing the clubhead*. Trumbull, CT: Golf Digest. (Original work published 1952)

Kostis, P., & Dennis, L. (1982). *The inside path for better golf*. Trumbull, CT: Golf Digest.

McCleery, P., & Cook, C. (1986). *Tips from the tour*. Trumbull, CT: Golf Digest.

National Golf Foundation. (1984). *Golf instructor's guide*. Jupiter, FL: Author.

National Golf Foundation. (1984). *Planning and conducting competitive golf events*. Jupiter, FL: Author.

National Golf Foundation. (1984). *Golf coaches guide*. Jupiter, FL: Author.

National Golf Foundation. (1984). *Golf lessons*. Jupiter, FL: Author.

National Golf Foundation. (1984). *Visual aids for golf instruction*. Jupiter, FL: Author.

Nicklaus, J. (1985). *The full swing*. Trumbull, CT: Golf Digest.

Nicklaus, J., & Bowden, K. (1980). *Play better golf*. New York: Pocketbook.

Nideffer, R. (1979). *The inner athlete: Mind plus muscle for winning*. New York: Crowell.

Owens, D. (Ed.) (1984). *Teaching golf to special populations*. Champaign, IL: Leisure Press/Human Kinetics.

Rotella, R., & Bunker, L. (1981). *Mind mastery for winning golf*. Englewood Cliffs, NJ: Prentice-Hall.

Runyan, P. (1979). *The short way to lower scoring*. Trumbull, CT: Golf Digest.

Simek, T., & O'Brien, R. (1981). *Total golf*. Garden City, NY: Doubleday.

Toski, B. (1978). *The touch system for better golf*. Trumbull, CT: Golf Digest.

Toski, B., & Flick, J. (1984). *How to become a complete golfer*. Trumbull, CT: Golf Digest.

Toski, B., & Love, D. (1988). *How to feel a real golf swing*. Trumbull, CT: Golf Digest.

Watson, T., & Hannigan, F. (1984). *The new rules of golf explained and illustrated*. New York: Random House.

Wiren, G., & Coop, R. (1979). *The new golf mind*. New York: Simon and Schuster.

Videotapes (VHS/Beta)

I. Currently available through Golf Digest Video Center, Box 395, Trumbull, CT, 06611-0395

Bob Toski Teaches You Golf

Golf Digest Learning Library
- Vol. #1 A Swing For A Lifetime
- Vol. #2 Find Your Own Fundamentals
- Vol. #3 Driving For Accuracy
- Vol. #4 Sharpen Your Short Irons
- Vol. #5 Saving Par From The Sand
- Vol. #6 Putting For Profit
- Vol. #7 When The Chips Are Down
- Vol. #8 Winning Pitch Shots
- Vol. #9 Hitting The Long Shots
- Vol. #10 Trouble Shots: The Great Escapes

Paul Runyan's The Short Way to Lower Scoring
    Vol. #1 Putting And Chipping
    Vol. #2 Pitching And Sand Play

II. Available through most local sporting goods stores and golf discount stores

Ben Crenshaw's The Art Of Putting

Sybervision
    Vol. #1 Al Geiberger
    Vol. #2 Patty Sheehan

Jack Nicklaus' Golf My Way

John Jacobs
    Vol. #1 The Full Swing
    Vol. #2 The Short Game
    Vol. #3 Faults And Cures

Wally Armstrong's Golf For The Kids

III. Available only through the National Golf Foundation, South U.S. Highway 1, Jupiter, FL, 33469

Golf Etiquette

How To Build Your Swing (Vols. 1 & 2)

How To Play Your Best Golf (Vols. 1 & 2)

IV. Currently only available through CHE, Inc., 222 East Bass Lane, Suffield, CT, 06078

Women's Golf
    Vol. #1 The Full Game
    Vol. #2 Short Approach

About the Authors

DeDe Owens, EdD, is the teaching professional at Cog Hill Golf Club in Lemont, Illinois, and a member of *Golf Digest's* instructional staff. A former professional on the Ladies Professional Golf Association tour, she holds the LPGA's Master Teacher ranking, having been cited as their Teacher of the Year in 1978.

In 1986 Dr. Owens received the Joe Graffis Award from the National Golf Foundation for her "outstanding contribution to golf education." This contribution has been made not only through her work as a club professional but also through her teaching at the University of North Carolina, Delta State University, Illinois State University, and the University of Virginia. Dr. Owens is also the author of *Golf for Special Populations* and co-author of *Golf: Better Practice for Better Play*, both published by Leisure Press.

Linda K. Bunker, PhD, is professor of physical education and Associate Dean for Academic and Student Affairs at the University of Virginia. She is a consultant for both the National Golf Foundation and the Ladies Professional Golf Association and is on the advisory boards of the Women's Sport Foundation and the Melpomene Institute, the Minneapolis-based research institute for women in sport.

In the Netherlands Dr. Bunker works as a consultant to the Holland Golf Team, and she has provided golf workshops for PGA professionals from Japan, Holland, and the United States. Widely published, she is the co-author of many other books, including *Mind Mastery for Winning Golf; Mind, Set and Match; Sport Psychology: Maximizing Sport Potential; Parenting Your Superstar;* and *Golf: Better Practice for Better Play*. A former nationally ranked junior tennis player, Dr. Bunker remains an avid tennis player when she is not on the links.